RANDOM THOUGHTS

DEAN SPARKS

ISBN-10: 148409672X
ISBN-13: 9781484096727

PREFACE

Random Thoughts is a culmination of discovery, reaction, and creation on subjects many of us ponder, then perhaps dismiss. But here, subjects of human thought, behavior, and emotion are approached through deliberate examination.

In this work, we find a range of topics including how we think, what role language plays in our thought process, as well as what roles imagination and creative powers play in that same process. Also offered are suggestions on making human behavior and human interaction more effective, along with practical suggestions on providing ourselves with safer travel, a smarter justice system, and better education practices. Ideas to improve our personal lives are also offered in areas such as health care, weight control, aging, and appreciation of the aesthetic.

In all, 490 ideas are compiled, with suggestions, explanations, and comments developed through logic and common sense. Each thought is a contribution to a larger conversation to which the reader will surely be compelled.

Conclusions are based on research and examination thus adding weight to the conclusions. The research employs works from those recognized academically in their fields, and serves as either starting points or worthy influences.

It is a process that considers the how, why, when and where, before declaring what. It certainly assumes the theory of evolution as based in science, and employs the strong influences of nature's survival of the fittest. With these assumptions, the book embarks on the logical unfolding that takes us to where we are today, and offers thoughts on where we may be headed.

With these assumptions, we are also aware that, although this work is entitled *Random Thoughts*, our present condition was more predictable than random. Indeed, this examination of the human condition has created a worthwhile read.

INTRODUCTION

A ubiquitous factor in the first manifestation of life on Earth was electricity. Essential to the function of the brain, evident in every part of the nervous system in addition to falling thunderously from the skies, electricity must have been extraordinarily impressive when Earth was new, as well as of calculable influence in the consequential occurrences in train at the time. The polar condition prevalent in electricity being negative in the earth, where life was in the fomenting stage, and negativity being consonant with a detracting modality, it is not surprising that the prevailing nature of evolving life in all its forms was and is of an evasive, defensive inclination, refined by cunning, and totally informed by determination to survive. In this modality, the evolving sensorium of all animals was necessarily sensitive totally to exterior situations. No faculty evolved for introspective communication; survival depended on constant vigilance. Thus the human brain evolved as a survival faculty, not a philosophical instrument. Extended thought (thought formulated by sequential images, each stimulated by a prior image and stimulating a following image) was undreamed of; short thought (sudden comprehension formulated by a single image guiding action) alone was possible.

The law of natural selection (my legislation) contains two conditions: a development it fosters (1) must be possible, and (2) must be given enough time to happen. 'Whatever can happen," the law reads, "given enough time, will happen." And so the forms of life that were more often able to detect the location and nature of a dangerous situation managed more often to survive to produce progeny like themselves; and this favoring of the intelligent and alert pretty well filtered out the stupid and inattentive. As frequent passage makes a path, interaction makes adaptation; and stimulation of cerebral cells forced cerebral formulation and adaptation while cerebral action brought nourishment by forcing increased blood flow. Nourishment stimulated the generation of new cerebral cells, the brain grew, and the intelligence of man increased.

From his very beginning (which took millions and millions of years) man used his ability to make sound with his breathing apparatus as he used his arms and legs; that is, to manage survival. Very gradually and largely unconsciously, he developed sound signals, every tribe a unique set of signals. This faculty gradually became speech; and with speech man developed a modicum of self control outmaneuvering his exterior-oriented mental faculties by the indirect method of his own audible or imagined vocal utterances taken in actually or imaginatively through his own hearing apparatus as instruction from an exterior source.

This private use of language was affirmed in the early nineteenth century by the eminent linguist Whilhelm von

Humboldt (1767-1835); and to this day, it is the most indispensable use man makes of language; for it undergirds thought, man's primary survival faculty. With language man gives thought a final formulation and holds thought in his consciousness until it can be used; and perpetual evolution has integrated language into the essence of thought, as evidenced by language's own special structures that have evolved within the brain exclusively for language's production (Broca's Area) and for language's comprehension (Wernicke's Area). Thus language gave man the gift of extended thought, of which I have made this book. Some of the thoughts herein are based on facts or theories originated by the scientific endeavors of persons learned in the germane subjects; some are of my own making.

These are thoughts. All I claim is that I thought them; I make few claims of proof. The reader must do his own thinking.

RANDOM THOUGHTS

1

One reason the brains of the aged become senile is that the disuse of brain cells, as has been proved tomographically, slows the blood whose increased rate of flow would provide nourishment for the generation of a greater number of new cells. To prevent the brain from becoming senile, one should exercise the brain by reading. The exercise of the brain is most effectively done by reading, no matter what one reads, because reading is a very complex process; and because words convey only ideas, the brain must create the imagery that initially formulates their meaning. By this creative exercise, the creative faculties of the brain are stimulated; and fresh blood is drawn in by the cerebral action, providing nourishment for a more rapid rate of cell generation.

2

The reason an old person's face looks old is the death of cells in the face muscles from lack of use. To keep or restore a youthful face, one should keep the face muscles built up by exercising them very strenuously once every day and letting them rest between exercises. The effect can be enhanced by following the exercise by gently kneading the face with the fingertips, causing subcutaneous displacement of stagnate blood and resurgence by fresh blood conducive to the generation of new muscle cells. For maximum effect, one should make this exercise part of one's morning toilet ritual indefinitely.

3

Our philosophy of human correction is anachronous. We still expect the guilty party to react to punishment like an animal; that is, to acquiesce and reform. We overlook the most important parameter in the matter of discipline, the reactionary peculiarity of the culpable party. The magistrate who must choose or approve the correctional measures should be allowed a psychiatrist to study the prisoner and advise.

4

When archaeologists discover a human track made three million years ago, they say that proves man was on the earth three million years ago. However, it proves much more than that. To evolve to the point that he could walk on two feet and leave a track that could be recognized as human took millions of years.

5

Learning is acquired by a plurality of presentations and reviews; that is, by rote. Rote learning was adopted centuries ago without the impetus of aversion to any other system of learning. It was adopted because it was seen to satisfy the requirements of learning. Our aversion to rote learning is based on our distaste for the boredom inevitable in repetition rather than on its inefficacy. The aspersing adjective unreasoning has no more affinity for rote learning than for the instrumentalist, behaviorist, or any other educational system. Reasoning also is learned by rote. In fact, all learning systems are effective only to the degree to which rote learning is embedded in them; for rote learning contains the quintessence of education, repeated presentation and review.

6

To show the advantage of repetition in learning, observe a child learning to operate a yo-yo. The child becomes very skilled very soon. Operation of the yo-yo quickly becomes second nature, habitual. This is because the child operates the yo-yo again and again—not because he knows how to learn, but because playing with the yo-yo is fun. This same principle, now that every child's desk is equipped with a computer, will enhance academic standards the world over; for the computer is the finest toy yet devised, and the most akin to the real world.

7

Repetition in learning is like Plutocracy in government: it's the quintessence of every system.

8

The reasons an artist's painting of a scene is more rewarding to scrutinize than a photograph of the real scene that the artist set out to paint are no doubt numerous. Edward Hopper said the photographed details are not heavy enough, and I believe that is one of the reasons. However, I believe the most significant reason was given by Gustaf Britsch almost a century ago. According to Britsch, any part of reality contains details that cannot be consistent with any imaginable work of art; and this is true because the details are not artistically consistent even among themselves. The view of reality may have given the artist his motif, but the artist has altered the view. The work of art he creates is not an imitation of nature. Though well aware that he has changed many details for artistic reasons, as a poet might use poetic license, he still considers the work an imitation. Instead, he has produced a creation of his own making in which every particular harmonizes with the intended unitary effect. And there are many such particulars, some of which many of the viewers may have no conception and that will stimulate their appreciation without their knowing the cause (see "A Neglected Theory of Art History," by W. V. Andersen, in *The Journal of Aesthetics and Art Criticism*, Volume 20, Issue 4).

9

The ultimate reduction: because things have to be different in order to be experienced, we have to experience them all with the same faculty in order to experience their differences. Since we know we have an imagination and do not know we have any intellectual modality for which the imagination cannot be used, we should realize our intellect consists entirely of our imagination.

10

If language is part of thought (and internalized language is the final formulator of all thought), then we can improve our intelligence by improving our knowledge and use of words.

11

Internalization of a physical action has occurred when one can perform the action without thinking of any of the details of it and when the body parts that perform the action seem to remember how to do it. An experienced bicyclist has internalized the action of riding a bicycle; an experienced dancer has internalized the actions of dancing. One has internalized a word when the meaning of the word functions in one's thoughts without one's being conscious of the actual word.

12

The reason a computer will never do what a human brain can do is that the computer and the brain function in different modes: fallible and infallible, the brain fallible; the computer infallible (see thought number 438).

13

Man's incipient evolution occurred in an environment of danger exterior to himself, and those of his species who survived to spawn progeny like themselves were those who the most diligently kept an outward-looking vigilance. No part of the brain developed for introversion. Later, when survival began to favor those with a modicum of invention and thought involving the self became advantageous, man, responsive only to exterior stimuli, utilized his own voice, reentering through his own aural faculties as stimuli from an exterior source, to communicate with himself; vocal signals gradually became speech; and language was born.

Man's outward-oriented mental faculties, sensitive to change in outlying conditions, allow him to think only relatively. He can recognize any entity only by comparing it to what it isn't. His inability to analyze directly his own brain disallows self-consciousness. He can be conscious of himself only as though he were another person, and he can judge another person only by comparing that person to other persons or things. To think of any entity in relation to other entities is to think analogically; analogy is the soul of invention; metaphor is the linguistic manifestation of analogy; language, the structure of meaningful thought, is a formulation of metaphors; and every word man utters, because it is an analogy in linguistic form, is an act of creation. For man, creation is inevitable; man produces inventions as a bee produces honey; he can make nothing else.

14

Man's immutable communication with himself as with another person renders him susceptible to self-alienation in some situations that threaten to expose something about him that he cannot countenance for shame or fear.

15

Man, having evolved totally intent on exterior hazards and therefore genetically unable to appraise his own brain directly, must talk internally to himself as to another person in order to think. Language, then, so integral to man's thought, is the essence of his intelligence and the proper study for his cultivation.

16

When one has just finished eating, one remains in the eating mode for quite some time. That is, one still feels a powerful impulse to eat. The reason for this is that, while one is doing anything, one's brain is remapping by weakening certain synapses and strengthening others in order to make the doing of the activity in progress easier, more effective, and consequently more enjoyable. If one begins to perform a different activity, the brain immediately begins to remap and adjust to facilitiate the doing of this new activity. Since the few extra bites one is tempted to take after eating a sufficient meal are the commonest cause of weight gain, it behooves one who is trying to lose weight to begin immediately after a meal to perform some activity that is not very vigorous and that is not related to eating. This is the quickest way to abate the eating mode.

17

One's every movement or thought is controlled by an opposing movement or thought, a cautionary inhibition that was evidently integrated early in man; for inhibitory neurons have been found at the synapses of the brain. When a thought is communicated, however, the controlling cautionary caveat is not communicated; and the recipient does not, as expected, accept the thought uncritically. Instead, he adopts it as his own in a critical spirit. Missing the controlling opposition, the recipient finds the communication lacks balance and feels a strong impulse to supply it. In this way, fortunately for the human species, a plurality of possible solutions to every critical problem that faces society is evoked.

18

Thought cannot be formulated by imagery alone; for images are not stable enough to carry thought cursorily. Such versatility is possible only with sound, because sound reverberates in the aural faculties and makes a memory in the mind that can last a lifetime.

Having the necessary stability, sound, the final formulator of thought must be able, audibly or imaginably, to represent a universe of different entities; and so sound, broken into words, each word given allegorical association with an item, condition, cause, or conception becomes a metaphor, and thought, through imagery, preinfuses man with a love of the visual arts and, through metaphor, with a love of the world of words.

19

The conditions of earthly nature has made necessary the existence of a single governing factor of every form of life and has limited that factor to power short of the destruction of the governed. Under this system of government alone can life exist on Earth. A governing power with the power of life and death over the governed would soon be destroying those with whom he differed, and difference of opinion is necessary for the survival of intelligent life because it effects the proposal of multiple solutions to critical problems. Therefore a muscle, if overtaxed, will stop responding to a cortical impulse short of serious injury; a political constituency will rebel short of total destruction; and even a rebelling mob requires an impromptu leader.

Hence there has never been a democratic government. Democracy has been feigned under cover of a confusion of government agencies, different ways of putting the government in power, and short terms of office; so that every type of government calls itself a democracy. Every people believes its government is a democracy, but harks to a law promulgated and enforced by a single unit of government as a guide to action.

20

The need to believe is a parameter of all consciousness because consciousness is a survival faculty, and, as a survival faculty, must reveal any need to take an action. The failure of consciousness to satisfy the most primitive creatures as to this need results in neurotic behavior. This is patent proof that any creature that has a brain, pace certain philosophers, is conscious.

21

We shape our tools, and our tools shape us. Language is a tool we use in thinking and expressing thoughts; therefore language influences what we think and how we think it. The word for strong, for example, influences one's idea of strength. The Arabic word for strong contains the sounds "azeeza," suggesting a squeezing, straining idea. The English "strong" suggests tension and leverage in the exercise of strength. The French "fort" suggests an idea of compact heaviness. The Spanish "Fuerte" suggests an idea of force accompanied by speed. People who learn one of these languages as a first language will have a different idea of strength than those speaking a different native language. Man's way of life is so influenced by the words he uses that each of these different ideas will have a general influence toward a different type of action in the exercise of strength.

22

Babies who, while still in the womb, hear their parents' voices will learn their native language more aptly thereby after birth; for the sounds will, to some extent, be remembered. But they begin unconsciously while still in the womb to create a private language, meaningful to themselves alone, in reaction to their instinctive urge to think and to control their situation in the interest of survival. This entails no impulse to speak aloud because the first and most important use of language is silent. Its function is to control thought. The impulse to audible speech will come with their discovery of their ability to make sounds with the speech faculties. The language they will learn will be decided by their imitation of their parents.

This opinion is arguable and much argued. I conceived my version of it by contemplation inspired by the researches of Aleksandr Romanovich Luria (1902-1977), Soviet biologist and author of *The Nature of Human Conflicts.*

23

We cannot conceive of anything we cannot express with words; for words, audible or imagined, are necessary to formulate and hold thought for our use of it.

24

We have learned that one's brain works by neural routing and synaptic adjustment to facilitate whatever one is immediately doing. This proves learning is habit formation and all experience is formative. It makes all we do important.

25

In order to be virtuous, we have to know the evil we would avoid. If we know the evil, we are capable of doing it and being in all ways variable, some will do it under certain conditions. If we do not know the evil, we are not virtuous, only innocent and while we would not know how to commit the evil, we would not know how to avoid it. For these reasons and also for the reason that inclination is volatile, Kant was right: duty, not inclination, should govern virtue. This obtains today in Japan, a very law-abiding country (see *Confucius Lives Next Door,* by T.R. Reid).

26

Insisting that children learn the rules that govern language while they are learning to read is hindering the child by doubling the task. Learning the rules is quite another matter than learning to read. We should allow the child to learn to read as he learned to talk, by imitation and habit formation (as indeed he will learn to read because he can learn in no other way). He will use the rules as he uses them in speech, before he learns they are rules. This is the way hyperlexic children learn to read—without learning a single rule. Their parents don't even know their hyperlexic child is learning to read. Teaching to read should consist of the parents reading to the child from matter the child enjoys. In school, the matter should be shown on a large screen with the moving image of a pointer pointing to each word as it is being pronounced. This will cause the pupil to concentrate on the word as he hears it spoken. Testing would be simply having the pupil read matter selected for the purpose.

27

In the mid-twentieth century several neuropsychologists discovered that the brain harbors efferent (out-bearing) neurons that don't carry impulses to muscles to instigate action as they were formerly thought to do. Instead, they carry impulses to spindles in which they meet impulses carried by afferent (in-bearing) receptor neurons and adjust these incoming impulses to accord with anticipated conditions and actions. This preparedness (dubbed by scientists "feedforward," as opposed to "feedback") allows us smooth and accurate actions, except when conditions are not as anticipated. An example of this misconception, given in Karl Pribrim, *Languages of the Brain,* instances an escalator that has unexpectedly stopped functioning. Stepping on this escalator, informed by feedforward that all is as usual and expecting to be carried rapidly upstairs, one nearly falls forward. One doesn't quite fall however, for it takes the brain only about half a second to correct feedforward.

28

Sometimes an error of feedforward is so slight that the contrast with reality is too negligible to stimulate the brain to correct it. In that case, the error persists, as when, because one has read a word wrongly, one remembers reading something and later cannot find it to confirm. Illusory images likewise depend on a too-slight difference between two different circumstances.

29

Feedforward is sensitive to mental action, a fact discovered by the German physicist Herman von Helmholtz (1821-1894), though feedforward as we know it had not become generally known at that early date. For example, I have discovered that feedforward reacts to imagination that is too slight to stimulate the brain's correction. One can look at a stationary ceiling fan, imagine it turning slowly clockwise, and it will appear to be turning very slowly clockwise. If one then looks at the fan to see if it is turning very slowly counterclockwise, it will appear to be turning very slowly counterclockwise. If one looks likewise intently at an inorganic black speck on a floor and thinks of it as an insect, it will soon begin to appear to be slowly moving. These illusions persist even though stationary objects near them prove they cannot be moving at all. In this case, one's imagination stimulates one's optic sense, but the movement one fancies one observes is too slight to stimulate a mental reaction. Thus is disorder enhanced which has enhanced man's adaptability through countless primordial catastrophes.

30

Man is a psychological animal. He can know anything only as it seems to him to be. He can be aware of only psychological time. To be aware of scientific time, he must use a clock; and he can understand scientific time only in psychological terms. This is one of the reasons every person lives in his own mental world, which is not the same as any other person's mental world.

31

Everything we know is fantasy; for we can take perceptions from only our senses, whether our sensations derive them from actual experience or only from imagined experience. Some things we don't have available to take repeated perceptions of, such as witches, ghosts, or second sight. These we believe on evidence that is itself fantasized. Scientific discoveries are available for us to take repeated sense impressions from and are believed on direct and immediate evidence. These we call proved. However, because we constantly build new fantasies around them, these proved matters are constantly being seen differently and are being proved again and again.

32

An overcrowded people isolate themselves by politeness. They nullify courtesy by its over-expression, which both incites and annuls resentment.

33

Everyone sees the world according to his own experiences, and no two people have had the same experiences. Therefore, though everyone lives in the same physical world, no two people in the entire world live in the same mental world. We see, feel, and otherwise sense everyone living in our physical world and assume that all live in our mental world also; hence the chaos of misunderstanding we all live among.

34

If one wants to become something for which one is fundamentally unfitted and has no talent, one should not, on that account, barring physical disability, stop trying to become that something; for while one is doing it, one's brain is making one fundamentally fitted for it, developing talent for doing that very thing.

35

Every plan must be utopian because to plan means to imagine ahead. The reality we must fit our plans to is necessarily a figment of our imagination. Our intent must be to join utopia and reality, realizing it is not quite possible.

36

I congratulate the author Frederick Reuss on having the protagonist in his novel *Horace Afoot* observe that a reader absorbed in a work of fiction feels himself actually to exist therein. This seems to be true of me. Reading *The Secret History* by Donna Startt, I was in the midst of a description of a windy autumn day, the wind blowing leaves into the characters' faces. I turned my head away from the window, then looked about in genuine surprise, realizing it was a very calm day, no wind, and no flying leaves. I had even heard the wind blowing the leaves against objects. What is more, I was reading indoors, with no windows or doors open.

37

The explosion of the space shuttle Challenger shortly after take-off with the loss of seven lives was an object lesson with the whole world watching that a deep study of bureaucratic management was in order. Subsequent investigations revealed the same symptoms that are in blatant evidence wherever bureaucratic procedures are used: lack of understanding between levels of authority.

38

One respect in which I feel the US educational system excels the Japanese is the attitude toward individual excellence. In the US, if a student proves outstanding, we give that student praise and encouragement. Conversely, the Japanese inform their students that an eminent student is like a nail that sticks up and must be driven down. I find Japanese art commensurate with this attitude in that, except in pictures of religious figures and royalty, it often lacks a central feature toward which the rest of the work directs attention.

39

The requirement of uniform cultural transmission that prevailed in the educational system of ancient Egypt may have survived through the centuries to its modem manifestation in the Japanese prohibition of individualism in their primary school years. This may mark a major difference between East and West.

40

The mind is the functioning of the brain, and attention is the limiting circumstance of the mind. It is peculiar that, with all the diverse and simultaneous functions of which the brain is capable, only a narrow and limited extent of them encompassed by attention can be functional at any one time. As the spotlight that directs and focuses the effectual activities of the mind, attention occupies a principal office in the operation of it.

41

The survival of a tribe, during the evolution of man, depended on the wisdom of its elders. The tribes with the wisest and most knowledgeable elders were the tribes that survived to have offspring like themselves. For this reason, learning in old age has necessarily become integrated into the genetic makeup of man.

More and more tribes with ability to learn in old age have populated the earth. Incredible as it may appear, therefore, it can hardly be denied that old age is perhaps not the best, but the most expedient time for learning.

42

Wisdom is knowing when to make an assumption.

43

We plan the construction of our highways with a view to the way drivers are supposed to drive, knowing full well the drivers will not drive as they are supposed to drive. We, ourselves, don't. When a driver crosses the double yellow line "for unknown reasons" killing himself and whatever innocent person or persons are in the vehicle he collides with, we feel a primitive little kernel of angry revenge. "He didn't drive as he knew he was supposed to drive," we say, "so what could he expect? If he had obeyed the law, there would have been no accident." The deaths of the innocent are considered an act of God, or briefly dismissed as a stroke of bad luck. We concede the axiom that "Everybody makes mistakes," but our road construction makes no allowance for mistakes. We do not allow for the consequences of sleepiness, road rage, fatigue, hungriness, etc. knowing beyond question that these affects will take their toll.

44

When one person gives another a bit of information, he does not give the other the same information that is in his own mind, but gives him instead a new bit of information. This is because words make the skeleton of thought, not the entire thought; and one can thus give only a part of what is in one's mind to anyone else (see pages 19 through 22 of Richard Semon's *Mnemic Psychology,* 1923). Hence the constant potential for creativity in the works of every person, even the least learned.

45

Difficulty in one's distinguishing the right or left side of a person facing one, due to one's having had difficulty learning to talk as a child, is proof of the critical involvement of language with thinking.

46

Every time a person, happening upon a desired lifestyle, deters further change in order to retain that preferred style, that desirable lifestyle starts to build resistance to itself like a grader blade at right angles with the line of advance accumulates excess of earth. Thus Hegel's dialectical thesis will always find its antithesis and will eventually necessitate a synthesis. Human predominance on Earth is no exception to this rule.

47

The mind is a survival faculty whose purpose is to protect. The uses of the mind depend on language, which is the model on which the mind builds extended thought. The cultural advance of earthly creatures depends on the improvement of their language and their use of it. Reading, writing, and rhetoric are therefore the most important studies in all academia.

48

The brain's survival function is partly affected by its communicative dysfunction, the inability to decode perfectly another's postulations, which fosters disagreement, causing many different solutions to be proposed for every civil problem, thereby increasing the chances of finding the best solution.

49

Too much of anything lowers its value in the opinion of its recipient, and the information glut caused by television lowers the value of information globally.

50

Man's cognition is based on sentiment; therefore television's balancing of pros and cons on every issue results in less of reasonable thinking than of indifference.

51

Nothing takes the mind away from reality so effectively as movies in a darkened theater; and they, by emotional incitement, invariable sanctify violence.

52

The use of words is a matter of making certain sounds to denote certain objects or conditions based on allusion to certain onomatopoeic or associative similarities between sound and object; which is to say all uses of words are metaphoric; and considering the fact that the use of words is essential to thought, we see an interesting relation between thought and metaphor.

53

The fonder we are of ourselves, the fonder we can be of others; for we realize others to the extent that we identify with them. When we identify with someone or something, that person or thing becomes a part of ourselves in a psychological sense; and they or it then share our esteem according as we esteem ourselves. We identify with other persons and things because they make us who and what we are. This is because nothing and no one is recognizable except by contrast with who or what they are not. It is therefore only by contrast with things that are not human that we are human. We therefore need the things and persons we contrast with. We need other persons because we have our personality only by contrast with other person-alities. The proof that we identify with the inanimate things is shown by the fact that, like primitive man, we get personally angry with an inorganic implement that seems to be trying to frustrate us in our use of it.

54

Earth creatures have only feeling, memory, and imagination with which to apprehend and appreci-ate life. Reason is only one of man's chimerical fanta-sies, an imaginary construct stabilized by language. Language is allowed man through memory; memory exists by virtue of time lag, by which two or more stimuli are made one. This sparsity of causal factors allows earthly organisms the ultimate versatility in environmental adaptation. The cumbersome super-fluity of distinct components the philosophers would have us consist of would leave us prey to the first change in the weather.

55

It might be possible to learn whether man, like the European weather fish *Misgurmus fossilis,* reacts to changes in barometric pressure by studying prevalent moods of people living on mountain sides in different isobaric areas. This knowledge would have value in situations common in the business world.

56

There is no reasoning in nature; nothing has been planned. Inertia, acted on by earthly conditions, has done all.

57

One of the things we should be trained in is the use of the stomach in performing only the needed nutritional function, not letting it take over our lives.

58

The frequency of misunderstanding in human interactions is evidence of the prominence of psychic engulfment, the erroneous belief that one's world is everyone's world.

59

In idle reverie, the human mind indulges in creative thought by virtue of the fact that one memory wakes another and in the same unguided and effortless way appreciates imagined events that might be caused by resulting conditions. Thus is the human mind creative by instinct, genetically inventive.

60

The more one's attention is kept on a worthy principle, the greater will be the influence of that principle on one's actions. This is demonstrated positively in Japan, one of the least crime-ridden countries in the world (see *Confucius Lives Next Door,* by T. R. Reid). Most anywhere one looks in Tokyo, according to T. R. Reid, one sees large signs espousing what we call the golden rule. The citizens of the United States supply a vivid inverse demonstration, in regard to crime, of the validity of this prescript, but validate it, perhaps even more effectively than Japan, by the millions they spend on advertising.

61

When one is in bed with nothing to divert one's feelings, a distressing memory affects one deeply, disabling sleep, because it shares one's attention with no other absorbing memory. One should read, then, to divert one's attention.

62

Every memory the mind acquires is fashioned partly by memories already in the mind and is therefore different from anyone else's memory of the same matter. This results in automatic creativity when two persons discuss any subject, for each receives original information from the other to process within the area of the influence of his own memories.

63

Painters who, like the poet Browning, fear producing work like other artists should consider the truth that every painting and every poem is unique. An artist in any mode of creation who allows the work of other artists to influence his own in any but a learning capacity is not practicing his art, but is like an animal in flight from a traveler who is not in pursuit. An artist should define his own concept of artistic creation and hew undistractedly to that line. Neither praise nor profit should swerve him in his course.

64

No earthly creature can think other than relatively, because there is no way the significance of any entity can be known except by comparison with what it isn't; and any entity, to be considered in any reasonable manner, must rest on a foundation of at least recognizable familiarity. Man cannot even think of a situation of which the adjective "absolute," in the sense of compared to nothing, would be distinctive. When one says absolute, one means more or less of some attribute relative to anything else in existence. Because to think of anything compared to nothing is redundant, every memory trace in any person's constellation of memory traces is constellated according to its value relative to all the others; and every concept any person acquires or creates must be mentally intro-jected into this constellation of memory traces according to its value relative to all the others. Thus every person has an accumulation of memory traces acquired in a lifetime's experiences and stored in a mental configuration accord-ing to that person's unique constellation of values.

Thus is human creativity ever inevitable due to the misunderstanding that prevails in all human interpersonal communication, for it is because no word means quite the same to any two persons that every person's constel-lation of memory traces is unique, and it is because the intellectual constituencies of no two persons have ever been shaped by the same formative experiences that no word stimulates the same train of thought in the minds of any two persons.

65

Our teaching runs counter to our learning, the teacher giving the student what the teacher knows. The student assimilates knowledge only according as he can understand it from what he already knows.

66

Thought is the interpretation of feeling by imag-ery which is given understandable and communicable form by audible or silent internalized language.

67

Good communication can best be achieved in a work of fiction when the author is least identified, so that the reader can entertain a subconscious feeling that the story is occurring in his own life.

68

If a parent praises his child as intelligent, the child will see himself as intelligent and will try to maintain that image in the eyes of his parent. If the parent calls his child stupid and punishes the child for his honest mistakes, the child will not think it worth the effort to try to be intelligent.

69

What we see depends not merely on what we see, but also on the light we see it in.

70

By keeping order in our material environment, we incline ourselves to an orderly way of thinking by transfer from material to mental.

71

Mathematics is not abstraction; like diction, mathematics is a bridge we use to carry us across the abyss of abstraction. We cannot think in the abstract.

72

Concepts acquired by watching television are easy to remember, for television impresses with both sound and sight; while reading requires the creation of imagery and internalized language to formulate the meaning of a code. All this laborious decoding, however, stimulates neuronal and synaptic action, nourishing cerebral blood flow, and consequent cellular generation; while television damps one's thought by stifling one's creativity under its infinitude of ready-made images, deadening one's mental action and allowing cerebral cells to die of disuse. Each mode has its use, but the enticements of television counsel control.

73

Thought is within the mind. When we think of something, we take it within the mind, which places it beyond the range of direct consideration. We have to see it indirectly; that is, in relation to other things. We have to learn how it is by the way it differs from other things. We think by such images as we identify with what we think about. Our lines of analogy are changeable, abstract, and obscure. Because thought is emotion, we identify with what we observe with attention. We can consider something only by considering ourselves in the likeness of it in form, situation, and intention. That is why primitive man believed insensate objects had feelings and intentions. He believed this because, when he thought of them, he took them in mentally, as part of himself; that is, he identified with them. We cannot directly consider what we think about because it is part of ourselves in a psychological sense, and our brain evolved as a monitor of external conditions.

74

The survival value of extended thought assured its saturation of the entire human species, and the fact that language is the only system that arranges concepts of infinite significance in a logical and cursive manner renders language a cofactor in the creation and utilization of extended thought. Because language was necessary for the evolution and functioning of the survival faculty of thought, it would early have attached to thought by genetic integration. Language can therefore be considered a part of thought, the framework of it, as the skeleton is the framework of the body.

75

To effectively teach someone, we must remember the student can't see things from the teacher's point of view. An infant must learn to walk with his own feet, and a student must comprehend instruction from his own point of view.

76

Language carries and guides thought. By carrying thought where thought would not otherwise go, language exposes thought to stimulations and inspirations that thought would not otherwise have experienced. After thought's birth through feeling and its initial development by imagery, language gives thought its final formulation for understandability by its creator's mental soliloquizing. Talking to oneself, in fact, is the most indispensable use of language. Many subhuman animals, having very primitive or no means of interpersonal communication, must yet soliloquize; for they are capable of such thought as is required in their econich.

77

Newborn thought is like a newborn human, who is capable of learning any language and adapting to any culture. The thought, conceived by a feeling, perchance, of ethics, esthetics, resentment, ambition, pity, or whatnot, will, after developmental roughing out by imagery and final evaluation and syntactic formulation by language, be a more or less different product than promised by its sentimental antecedent. Like a child, born with only bestial instincts for survival, after early socialization and some little training, the new thought will be soon seasoned in the remembered experiences of its progenitor. Like the communication of thought, the attempt to generate it pure and true is not an option.

78

Thought is the evaluation of concepts.

79

Samuel Johnson, asked to prove the invalidity of solipsism, said, "I prove it thus!" and kicked a stone violently. It is surprising that a man of his culture and creativity did not think to say, "When I remember something as being a certain way and find it not that way at all, but another way, that proves reality is determined by something other than my mind, disproving solipsism."

80

The brain is the most important survival faculty of every organism that has a brain, and every organism that has a brain is capable of imagining, for the only use that can be made of a brain is imagination.

81

Primarily, man has only feelings. His feelings transmute to imaginiation. His imagination is analogous to a bulletin board on which any concept can be displayed and considered. Hence philosophy's superfluous distinctions.

82

Every decoding is another encoding; that is, the comprehension of proffered information entails the recipient's revision of it according to his own cognitive schema. This encoding is habitual. Like the necessary assumptions we have to make every day, it is often used excessively; by dent of which we find others thinking we said more or less than we actually said.

83

Sometimes in my travels I have come to a place where I say, "What a beautiful place! I love this place!" And what have I done to so appreciate it? I have seen it. What I have felt or otherwise sensed there I can experience most anywhere. Just so do I sometimes see a painting of a place and thrill to its beauty even more than I thrill to the actual place; for to enhance the single effect the artist has intuitively deemed most charming for that place, whether directly, or relatively by altering some item near it, the place the artist has created has been transformed in every detail. I have learned that if a painting that so thrills me is for sale and I don't buy it, it may haunt me till I decide I must have it; and when I return to make the purchase, I will likely find it gone. Ever after, the memory of that painting may haunt me as a bit of wonderland that I have lost, never to find again.

Many years ago a painting in the window of a thrift shop held me enraptured a moment. Returning next day, I found it gone. I don't remember the subject painted, only the frustrated desire. I could have had it for a dollar, and I still grieve a little for the loss of it. It was a small painting, maybe ten by twelve inches; and it was a predominantly golden brown color. There were some trees in it, and subdued sunlight. It taught me life is not so long that we can pass these golden moments by.

84

Communicative language was not invented; it developed subconsciously and gradually; that is, it evolved. Its great survival value integrated it from the very beginning into the human genetic constitution. Subject, verb, and object represent the thing that acts, the act, and the thing acted on that are so prominent in experience; and the syntactical order of the words is dictated by the natural order of the actions. Language is the mental parallel of action. Physical action is the hard core around which language has grown and taken shape. Language took the shape of action as naturally as snow takes the shape of the scape it covers. Where action was accompanied by sound, language mimicked the sound; for mimicry, because it can form habits, is a valuable learning tool; and this mimicry of otic experience portends that syntax took form by the mimicry of the action inherent in all experience. All languages exemplify this.

85

There are many languages; for through the millions of years of tribal living, every tribe developed its own language, or, splitting from its parent tribe, gradually altered its native language. This latter process (linguistic drift) is in effect now, in the Brazilian rain forest, where nearly every tribe has its own unique language. It's also in effect in civilized languages, only slower.

86

Everything one knows is interconnected with everything else one knows. The brain contains a constellation of items of knowledge, and everything one learns must be fitted into this constellation according as one feels its value compares with the value of all the items already placed. Thus everything one learns occasions a repositioning, however slight, of every item in the constellation of one's items of knowledge. The brain is not an organ of interconnected parts; the brain is an organ consisting of one part that consists of many subsections, each of which subsection consists of a neuronal route; and every subsection, by means of reentry [the immediate firing back over every sensed neuronal route] is affected by every stimulative impulse experienced by any other subsection.

This hypothesis is substantiated by the fact that every part of the body, like every part of the brain, that is sensified by a stimulus affects every other part of the body, however slightly. This affect is most evident when the sensifying stimulus is extremely painful or extremely pleasant. And this same fact further points to the cause of the phenomenon of consciousness, which is realized when reentry is given time by sense lag to resensitize every sensation of the brain, thereby effecting consciousness, the sensing of sensation.

Still further, the above described action, if we add the fact that learning is habit formation, makes very probable a commonsense cause that one's learning a new language grows more difficult with one's increasing age. The process of time, adding items to one's constellation of knowledge, both intended and inadvertent, soon makes quite a large constellation of items, each implanted by a degree of habitual usage, and all of which make a load that becomes more and more difficult of readjustment by a brain made constantly more diminished by selective disuse.

87

As a medium for interpersonal communication, language, though necessary, is used only sporadically and to little effect. A respondent is more likely to oppose than to approve one's opinion. Moreover, in interpersonal use language is ambiguous; for every person's mind-set is unique; and every person gives every concept unique meaning and value. In self-counseling, on the other hand, language is efficient and clear; for then the communicator and the communicatee are one and the same. In these conditions the principle use of language is implied. It is to make thought intelligible by formulation and to hold concepts in the mind long enough to allow consummation of the thought process. Man is in charge of himself every hour of his life; and thought is his most effective survival faculty as well as his most effective faculty for solving the problems of everyday living. That the formulation of his own thought is man's most indispensable use of language is further indicated by the fact that subhuman animals may lack interpersonally communicative speech, yet obviously think, manifesting a private language.

88

It is because, for us, all things are relative that every new concept we conceive has to be fitted into our constellation of values according as its value compares with our other concepts. That is also the basis for Richard Semon's theory that the communication of diverse experiences makes people misunderstand one another and gives their thoughts an inevitable creativity. Diversity of formative experiences causes misunderstanding between two conversants because it allows no word to suggest quite the same train of thought in the minds of any two persons and it impels creativity because it introduces new and unintended concepts into new and different constellations of value.

89

Because every person has a distinct brain, every person must conceive all his experience from his own point of view. He cannot have another person's experiences nor think with another persons' brain. He cannot, by listening to another person's words, understand from the speaker's point of view; he can reconstruct the speaker's experience only from his own point of view. Thus he can imagine the speaker's experience only as it would evoke memories in his own brain. This makes it an entirely different experience. It also causes any group of individuals to constitute a creative situation.

90

Since language is present in every occasion of thinking, language contains one's entire repertoire of suggestible concepts. The use of language is therefore very stimulating to one's thinking faculty.

91

Retrograde amnesia, by which memory is lost of a space of time immediately before brain injury, is indication that the mind requires a space of time thoroughly to realize and to assign an acceptable status for new concepts among infixed beliefs. Accordingly, returning to a book after a brief interruption, I always find I was reading a few lines lower on the page than I thought I was, showing that the memory of the last few seconds of my reading before my interruption was wiped out. Reading rapidly, our attention is taken from one concept to the next before the first can be fully registered in the mind, wiping the first, if we are interrupted, from the memory. I don't know if learning theorists have ever taken this under consideration. I've never read of it. The time it takes the mind thoroughly to integrate a mental impression is not known, I believe; but from my own experience with ether-induced general anesthesia, which also causes retrograde amnesia, I think the mere removal of attention would back the memory up from three to five minutes. The loss of memory from brain injury varies according to seriousness of the injury; the more serious the injury, the greater the loss; and according to a friend of mine who suffered such an injury, the time obliterated from the mind can be as much as one hour. Simply removing the attention prematurely from one concept to another, however, would probably cost the minimal memory loss, on interruption, leaving enough of the context uninterrupted that inference from remaining memory would effect what would amount to a recognition memory, making the material much easier to learn on a second attempt. This is the more likely considering that separation of study periods by a day or two is the most effective way to learn because of the extra stimulation occasioned by reapproachment after a period of quiescence.

92

To save evolving encephalonized animals from the hungry monsters then extant, the only feasible resource must have been superior intelligence; for no form of violence they could then have mustered would have deterred the hazards they faced. So every time genetic recombination produced a more intelligent animal, that animal's chances of surviving were a little better than the chances of any of his less intelligent fellow animals; and his contribution to the gene pool allowed more animals with brains to survive.

At last there evolved in every encephelonized earthborn animal a brain quite independent of the body, a brain that grew faster than the cranium that contained it. The animals of earth, along with their means of survival, had thus to accept a fatal flaw: someday their brains would be too tight in their crania to support life, or if the head grew larger it would soon preclude birth.

The killer whale, for example, has evidently been extant much longer than man; for its brain is obviously much tighter than man's, being much more wrinkled except in the lower parts, where the wrinkles have been quite pressed out. Man, to my limited knowledge, seems next in line for this honor of longest duration of earthly tenancy. Just how it came about, I propound a probable cause; but the fact that the brain grows faster than the cranium neuroscience has now made certain.

93

All life on this planet must have evolved, generally, by the same process as man, its principal parameters probably starting in particles of matter far smaller than the atom. The brain's growth and the cranium's constraint, barring more likely cessation, will be the fatal flaw of life on Earth.

94

Regarding a judge's instructions to a jury, in communication one must take into consideration both the sending and the receiving capacities involved. The judge looks back on educated parents, a childhood in a nice home filled with books, followed by a degree in law school. The average juror may or may not have a high school education and comes from a home of uneducated parents with all the everyday exposure to ignorance that implies. His vocation may require very little knowledge or training useful to a juror. He puts a meaning on the instructions different than the judge intends. An analogy might be that of a radio broadcasting station capable of sending in frequencies ten to twenty sending messages to a receiving set capable of receiving in frequencies three to five.

95

We like to read authors we agree with, not only because they write what we believe, but also because they write what may be an extension of what we believe. They help us think by offering us a "leg up," giving us either the next step in our thinking ready-made or starting us on a new train of thought. Reading an author whose thinking is antagonistic to ours will not help as much, though in the counter arguments that come to mind as we read we may surprise an idea that sparks a flame in the tinder of our intelligence.

96

All of life is process. We cannot stop a time of happiness and hold it for pleasure. We cannot say, "This is *now!*" For the infinitesimally thin slice of time that is the present, if there *is* a present, has become the past by the time we have thought to try to feel it as the present. One reaches out and finds nothing. One grasps at a solid present time to hold it and to better realize it just for however brief a moment, a second or a fraction of a second, and one's hands grasp thin air. The future is coming by and sweeping the present into the past, and we can only look back at the *now* that is now the past. There is no *now*.

We seek happiness by trying to grasp the present and hold it steady and say, "I am happy." We try to believe we can keep this happiness as long as we wish by holding this *now* indefinitely. But seriously and privately we know we have never experienced the present, that the *now* has eluded us and has always been gone when we turned to it and has left us feeling it was not something we saw but something we only *thought we* saw and could never *fix* our gaze on, could never look directly at. And we have rarely been happy when we meant to be.

We cannot have the present. It is never to be ours. To find happiness we must seek it in something we have. Life is a continual process and nothing stays the same for even a second. We must therefore seek happiness in process, or in looking to the future or the past. At the times when happiness has surprised us like an unexpected ray of light, what was its cause? Where did it enter our lives? Did we find joy in process, or in looking forward, or in looking back?

97

We enjoy the painting of an unremarkable scene because the artist has intuitively given it visual meaning by altering details to accord with the one visual expression intended (see "A Neglected Theory of Art History," by Wayne V. Andersen, in *The Journal of Aesthetics and Art Criticism,* for summer, 1962).

98

One can see how different one's world is from the world of anyone else by noticing how different is a drawing of some story character from the likeness one would make of that character if one could draw.

99

Ernst Cassirer (1874-1945), in his *Essay on Man,* gives man's mental faculties too great a part to play by dwelling on man's Greek legacy of valuing obedience of himself and coming suddenly vis-a-vis Christianity's ordinance to obey only God. Man's business has been principally to survive; and to manage this, he had not only to arrange matters physically to be able to acquire food and other necessities; he had also to arrange his mind to coincide with the necessary intentions and actions, for he had acquired a mind as well, with its inherited feeling for others and fear of their intentions.

I don't think man suffered much from this reversal of ecclesiastical philosophy. I think he transformed smoothly from one way of thinking to two, contradictorily enjoying both philosophies. After all, church was somewhere to go on Sunday. What man was worried about was money (see *The illustrated Chronicles of Matthew Paris: Observations of Thirteenth-Century Life*).

100

Natural selection has made many intricate and wonderful things because everything that can happen, given enough time, will happen. The human eye, often cited in this connection, is one of the things that could happen.

101

I believe a time that was not happy can become a happy time in memory. It may even have been an unhappy present time; but memory has suppressed the unhappy conditions that prevailed during its currency and has unconsciously patinated it with traces of other happy memories of similar times. We say, "I remember a happy time"; but it was not a happy time. It is happy only now, in memory.

But where else can happiness be found? We are what we believe, and all belief is memory.

102

If we have self-esteem, we got it of our parents through their precept and example. When we were tiny our parents were to us a man and a woman who *could do anything* and who *knew all. We* had no one in a like position with whom to compare them. If a thing they taught us was unpleasant, we had to accept it. With our limited experience, we had no alternative opinion. If we were one year old, a lifetime was one year; if we were five years old, it was five years; and the whole of this lifetime was filled, horizon to horizon, with these two super people. We were what they taught us to be, advertently by precept and inadvertently by example. They could not fail to teach us; because, though they might withhold the precepts, that most effective teacher of all, example, they could not withhold. If they showed us affection, were always ready and eager to give us approving attention, and only reluctantly disapproved of what we did, and then only with good reasons which we could understand and which they made sure we *did* understand, they taught us we were worthy of affection and respect. They made us feel good about ourselves and thereby gave us self-esteem as well as the distinguishing characteristic of respecting those with whom we identify. If, on the other hand, they showed us no affection and were eager to disapprove of what we did, they robbed us of our self respect and our future offspring and wives and husbands of our esteem.

103

All our attempts to improve government and society have been attempts to appease collective inclination. The problem is that inclinations are neither stable nor uniform. The volatility of inclination is nicely demonstrated by the establishing of bureaucratic procedures. All procedures look fine in theory, but the difficulties experienced in applying them soon has the committee writing a new procedure, which is preempted after a short term of use due to difficulties of its own. Conversely, as observed by Immanuel Kant (1724-1804), duty is stable; and the only way an ethical society will ever be established is by persuading it to consider ethical behavior a duty.

104

Lying in bed between sleep and waking, we reexperience the events of childhood, even in our old age; and our hearts quake again with the affects of inexperience kept fresh within us all this time.

105

Iphigenia was going to be sacrificed so the gods would give the Greeks a good wind to sail to Troy. Query: why did the people suppose the gods would want that lady to be killed? The answer to this might help us understand how people could think the death of Jesus would please God.

106

The European weather fish *Misgumus fossilis* shows changes in activity in response to changes in barometric pressure. I believe human beings respond to these changes, too, in mood. There are days when everyone frowns and other days when everyone smiles.

107

One is different at different times and often finds one's conclusion drawn earlier to be wrong; in light of which one's dudgeon on being found wrong by others, who are always different than one, is evidence of egotistically skewed judgment.

108

Wisdom is not intelligence, knowledge, or virtue. All these can be found in a fool. One's wisdom is one's ability and inclination to use the knowledge one has in an effective way to achieve an objective commensurate with the values physically and mentally conducive to the contentment of one's self and species.

109

The exercise of the imagination is the only function of which the brain is capable, for we have to use our imagination to appraise what we sense in reality as well as what we fantasize. The person, therefore, whose childhood is so circumstanced by loneliness or by parental encouragement as to effect a great use of the imagination is, because of this exercise of the creative faculties, in the condition most likely to develop the maximum degree of intelligence of which his or her brain is biogenetically capable.

110

Good fiction can be more affecting than a good movie because written narrative involves the reader by leaving to him the necessary creation of imagery; and to the same effect, the author evokes in the reader the maximum degree of identification by allowing the reader time to integrate maximally every narrated situation into the reader's constellation of values.

111

An author appeals to a reader's feelings indirectly by virtue of which the author evades the opposition factor. The reader's involvement through his creation of imagery makes the text, in large part, the reader's creation. The only opposition that occurs, therefore, is the controlling self-opposition that occurs in all thinking.

112

There's a wavering borderline between free enterprise and crime. They are so similar that one suggests the other and is a standing temptation.

113

If one is bored and tired of reading, words can become of so little import to the reader that they can no longer correct a mistakenly-anticipated expression.

114

The discovery that axons in the brain grow more dendrites to accommodate synapses for the management of increased knowledge is evidence that mind and body are two ends of the same thing, for it shows that mind and body grow as one to accommodate the increase of knowledge.

115

There's a disparity apropos of affectation vis a vis perspicacity such that the cleverest pretense of the local savant is transparent to the town simpleton. It's easy to believe we have an instinct to detect deceit, and that could be so, for such competence would have survival value. I believe, however, we all act mostly to experience our own satisfaction; and the ego of the observer is unencumbered with the self-directed cathexis that distracts the self-concerned pretendant.

116

The fact that some people's belief is based on faith instead of knowledge and who cannot be influenced by an argument based on knowledge indicates that humans can believe what they do not know is true. It also indicates that their sense of reason doesn't permeate their entire awareness. I agree with Wilhelm Dilthey (1833-1911) that humans are not primarily rational animals. I can think of nothing in the account of evolution that would tend to make them so. I see reason as a human invention useful in the justification of man's desires.

117

The fact that an imagined event has the same emotional effect on one, albeit less vivid, as the real event, has a fortunate corollary for application on blue days or nights when one's thoughts seem always to be drawn to depressing memories. One can moderate one's depression by vividly imagining remembered happy events. Describing the happy events in writing intensifies their imagination.

118

Whatever we do, our brain simultaneously adjusts throughout by neuronal rerouting and alteration of intensities to make us more proficient at that action and make the action, incidentally, more enjoyable. The result of this is that we are soon in the mode for performing that action. This phenomenon is most evident in relation to sleep in the morning and to eating after a meal. We are sleepier in the morning after a good night's sleep than we were at retiring the night before and have a greater desire to eat after a sufficient meal than before. This sequence must be controlled. It functions in everything one does, from thinking to doing; and like many effective agencies, it can do harm as well as good.

119

One must make one's decoding of someone else's encoding one's own encoding in order to understand it. Since no two think alike, there is no way one can learn from someone else. One can understand only oneself.

120

I would get what I would agree to call knowledge from induction by determining a standard number of experiments which I would call proof if the experiments found a situation to be true the standard number of times. This is in fact what we necessarily do. We never get closer to proof, for everything we know is based on induction.

121

Feeling is the basis of man's mentality. Feeling is the seed, imagery is the substrate, and speech is the florescence of thought. Man's intelligence is his management of his feeling. The caterpillar that reacts when one touches it with a twig has all man's mind in small.

122

Any form of naturally evolved life is more like a jellyfish than a well-oiled and precisely functioning machine. How we puff ourselves up!

123

A word that comes easily to one's tongue when one is not searching for it often escapes one when one is searching for it. Why is this? I believe it's the same or a similar phenomenon as addiction. One gets so inured to the use of the word that he becomes insensible of it. Asked where W is on the typewriter, the typist cannot say; the memory has gone into her fingers. This theory is commensurate with that of the memory of the aged being overcrowded.

124

We mentally accept our silent soliloquy back into our brain through our auditory sense as stimulation from an exterior source, and this activates the opposition factor the same as if it were really from an exterior source; for just as we always move under the control of opposing muscles, we always think under the control of opposing thoughts.

125

Apes lay up spare grass stems, used to catch termites, against future scarcity; ergo, they think; and the more astute gain a Darwinian survival advantage. This makes it certain that, if Darwinism is valid, the apes will eventually be as intelligent as humans are now.

126

A scene an artist is painting is like a group of unrelated words that make no sense; the artist's portrayal is like those words meaningfully arranged.

127

How will life on Earth end? There are many ways, any of which are sufficient; but its most likely end will be when Earth runs out of water. We have had a good look at Mars and Venus. They are devoid of life and full of dry river beds. So will Earth become.

128

Most onomatopoeia is on a secondary basis, word and referent getting their similarity from association rather than from sound or synesthetic suggestion. A word sounds like an entity appears or functions because it has always evoked the image of that entity; and this association has reinforced association with words usually appearing with it, cementing the primary association. For native speakers, similarity by habitual association is quite as valid as similarity by sound; for the suggestive connection is as evidently there.

129

It is because of consciousness as defined by Locke (the perception of what passes in a man's own mind) that we see ourselves as two beings, a body with a mind and an overviewing mind. Due to consciousness we can talk to ourselves.

130

The will is intention stirred to the point of action by immediate enticement and/or revivified memory and tempered or encouraged by consideration of related circumstances. The decision to act or abstain is made by the mind, which is the functioning brain. Very many immediate enticements that affect to a degree the intention and that might have culminated in action or forbearance at the instance of the will are ignored by the mind as not sufficiently related to other memories germane to the issue in question to stimulate action. These enticements lose their potency and die out. This and other decisions related to the action of the will are made by the mind. If the reasons the mind makes one decision instead of another are to be considered evidence that the will is not free, it leaves the will only two motives for action: predetermination and absurdity. The same can be said for the farmer's decision to plow his land, for the judge's decision to sentence a felon, for the pilot's decision to wait out a storm. The mind must weigh and consider before taking action in view of all its knowledge and accumulated experience. If all man's actions were predetermined, he could make no mistakes, at least no intentional mistakes. If all his actions were chosen at random, at least half of his actions, including his intentions, would be mistakes. As it is, most but not all of man's actions are not mistakes. If he is faced with a confusion of determinants, he has, at least, to decide which determinant to act on. The mind is limited, and there are so many causes to take one action instead of another that a limited mind cannot keep track of them. Instead, it must make its own decisions as to such causes as it determines to be of sufficient consequence to merit action. I submit the mind is an independent judge and the will is free.

131

The exercise of one's will is the effect of commands issued by one's brain. It might be said that something caused one's brain to decide to issue each of those commands, but the commands originated in one's brain, and the brain's instigating action for no reason would be insanity.

132

Reading is the best exercise for developing and preserving mental competence, for words convey only ideas, and we think with imagery. To understand words, we have to create mentally the images they signify. Reading thus exercises and preserves the neurons and synapses in the brain that generate creative thought and that, without exercise, wither and die.

133

Deferred punishment of crime assumes in the perpetrator a self-control in reaction to stimuli remote in time. The judge who sentences him and the members of the judiciary who write the laws are thoroughly capable of self-control in response to remote motives, a faculty acquired through mastery of language and a youth spent under the tutelage of highly educated parents. The perpetrator of crime, however, who is expected to use this sentence to inspire a distaste for crime, grew up in a home that contained no books, learned a vocabulary half of which consisted of curse words, and was taught nothing at home. He received his formative experiences while learning to avoid provoking an emotionally infantile, brutal, and alcoholic father (more likely a stepfather). Any event, of whatever consequence, that was to happen more than twelve hours in the future was not worth serious consideration. A court hearing six months after his arrest has no real relation to the crime in his eyes, but is only one of the high-executive procedures from which he can deduce no meaning. Had he been whipped immediately on the discovery of his guilt, he might have been brought one small step nearer to reform.

134

It has been thought that languages progress from complex to simple and that this indicates more sophisticated speakers during the earlier era of a language. It is more likely that speakers in the primitive era had not yet conceived of the convenience of categories and abstractions, and the supposed complication consisted of concretion and particularities.

135

The factual and the fictional are equal in the mind of man. It is in his imagination that he appreciates both. His assumption of them as different is also imagined, for it is in his imagination that he contemplates either and his reactions to either are the same.

136

Man in his tribal days lived much in the society of his fellows for safety's sake. He evolved as a social creature, guiding his actions and reactions by the immediate reactions of his fellow men. He is genetically a seeker of good companions.

137

Feedforward (being informed of one's immediately impending circumstances) can distort one's memory due to the consideration of preferred circumstances. One imagines the preferred conditions, and imagined experience is but a short remove from actual experience. Preferred displaces actual.

138

When one is reading rapidly, feedforward often makes one see--actually see—a word that, though expected, is not there. This is because the brain requires about a half-second to process and react to new information; and feedforward, preparing one for a next move or thought, conjures fleeting anticipation and imagery so intense as to approximate hallucination. (See Robert Pollack, *The Missing Moment,* pages thirty-eight and forty.)

139

It's language that gives man his intelligence, and so it's reasonable that the limits of language and man's measure of skill in the use of it puts the limit on man's intelligence. In addition, technology speeds up everyday activities, which causes people to have less time to spend on communication. There's a great need of improvement in interpersonal communication; misunderstanding is currently its commonest feature.

140

When I consider my accomplishments in life, I note principally that I have learned to read. I have learned to see and feel life through the printed word.

141

One may find little of interest in a book that, a few years later, may interest one a great deal. The book has acquired interest because it has changed in relation to the reader; the reader has grown mentally by developing new areas of interest.

142

There can be a science of esthetics. A rose appeals to bees visually and through the sense of smell, and bees are genetically programmed to appreciate the rose through these two senses. Both the rose and the bees got that way through the process of natural selection, the rose getting its pollen distributed and the bees getting nectar for honey. They got that way because those who were not that way didn't survive. So we can understand that all beauty is not in the eyes or nose of the beholder, at least some of it is in the genes of the beholder, at least with bees.

Query: can this also be the case with human beings? What is there that we call beautiful, the appreciation of which is conducive to our survival? To us the composed and smiling face that has even and proportionate features suggests friendliness and therefore possible help and safety through cooperation and sympathy. This situation is heightened by the fact that a distorted, hate-filled face means danger and lack of sympathy. This condition would spread to other situations by association and analogy, such as a beautiful day vs. a stormy day, an evenly-proportioned flower or object vs. its opposite, etc. The survival value of this would quickly become integrated into the human genetic make-up. Thus we can say the human appreciation of beauty, in its principal and primary parts, is not in the eye of the beholder. In the disorderly fringes, every person is unique; but, in the main, we all appreciate the same qualities. A good example of the appreciation of the sense-satisfaction serving as a survival faculty is the assembly of large taste buds in the shape of a V on the back of the tongue. The point of the V is down the throat a way, inducing one to swallow. The buds are sensitive to sweet and bitter. And it is through them that we derive much of our pleasure of eating. We are genetically programmed to appreciate the beauty of taste, which helps to assure that we will take nourishment; and because of this condition we can make a science of food preparation. As with our appreciation of physical beauty, some of our appreciation of food is unique; but, in the main, we all appreciate the same foods. It is for this reason that we can prepare and sell some kinds of food in large quantities: bread, fruit, candy, etc.

143

Some connecting factor that joins the entities together in a function is necessary to make a group of anything more than the sum of its parts. For example, four steel balls and four short chains are simply four steel balls and four short chains; but fasten one end of each chain to a separate steel ball and the other ends of the chains together, and you have a bola, which possesses a potential that is lacking in the unconnected four steel balls and four short chains. With a bola you can entangle a large animal long enough to capture it.

Analogously, if they know how to work together, a group of persons working together have powers greater than their total, working separately. Working together to solve a problem, each member of the group builds on what the others have found. Therefore, by not expressing the balancing agonistic thoughts that give credence privately to one's opinions, each member of the group is stimulated to restore the balance by expressing opposing thoughts. The disparity, in addition, of background among the individuals in the group broadens their resource of experience and gives further impetus to opposing viewpoints and consequent diverse solutions, improving the chance of success.

144

If the upper and lower parts of a number three are almost closed loops, feedforward may let one see it as an eight. If one tries, one can see the figure as either a three or an eight. However, if the loops of the three are a little more open, one cannot see it as an eight even if one tries. This minute difference reveals the amount of imprecision endowed man by natural selection, enhancing the disorder that in past cases of environmental change have sufficed for his survival.

145

A name signifies only one of the many aspects of the object named. Ernst Cassirer, in his book, *An Essay on Man*, page 134, explains that the ancient Greek name for the moon, "men," refers to the moon as an instrument for measuring time. The Romans called the moon "Luna," meaning bright and lucid. It's easy to understand from this that people speaking different languages live in different worlds.

146

All animals think creatively because they think with words or substitutes for words; and every word, because it is similar by customary association to its referent, is a metaphor. A metaphor is the expression of an analogy, and analogy is the algorithmic key to creation. Man must think by analogy because his brain evolved as an out-looking faculty. This faculty is out-looking because all of every animal's dangers were exterior to the animal's body and were so constantly imminent as to necessitate constant vigilance. Because man has no capacity for introversion, he cannot communicate directly with his own brain. He must do all his thinking by comparing exterior phenomena, by finding similarities; that is, by analogy; and analogical thinking is creative thinking. Considering the only way man can think is creative, it's not astonishing that his inventions are incredibly ingenious. They will become more so as the creative mode gradually intercalates the inventive genius into his genes. This process will gain speed with growth.

It's imperative that we set this modus operandi to work in man's ethical domain.

147

One can learn to not know something by experiencing the need to know it but not looking it up. The more times one does this, the more likely one is to do it again; for learning is habit formation and habit formation is learning. If at last one finds this evasive something in a reference work, one may very soon revert to not knowing it, having previously learned so well to not know it.

148

An increase in thought-provoking environmental features has proved to cause more synaptic connections to develop in the brains of animals, including man. This is the reason a person who keeps his mind active retains his intelligence in old age. If he does not use his brain, it will deteriorate.

149

If one can get to sleep, the brain will put itself in the sleep mode, one will be likely to remain asleep for some time, and one will be able easily to go back to sleep soon after waking. The brain will support the sleep mode as soon as one becomes sleepy, just as the brain supports the mode of anything else one is immediately doing.

150

The effect of simply closing one's eyes has never to my knowledge been recognized as soporific, but has been considered rather the effect than the cause of sleepiness. There seems to me, however, to be a neuronal connection between the muscles around the eyes and the sleep centers of the brain, similar to that between the muscles of the tongue and the muscles of the throat which enable one to swallow by sucking on the roof of the mouth (assuring nourishment for newborns). Any normal person whose despair of sleep is not the result of any exceptionally disturbing problem will find that by keeping one's eyes closed and concentrating on the comfort of lying in bed is the best way to find sleep.

Two concurrent conditions must be observed: one must keep one's mind in repose and one must keep one's eyes closed. Even the slightest glimpse after a period of closed eyes will destroy the entire effect so far accrued. Once the pump of sleep has been effectively primed, however, the brain will shift to the sleeping mode and a good night's sleep will be in prospect.

151

What is a novel supposed to do? A novel is supposed to entertain and give the reader concentrated vicarious experience such as might make him wiser in the conduct of his life.

152

There are two all-affecting factors: process and time. Everything that exists is in the process of changing all the time. Nothing stays the same for a second. Time doesn't pause for a present; it gives us only an ever-moving past and future. We have to pretend a present. We are thus anachronous in everything we do, for time won't wait. Life on Earth has developed understandably with this misbelief 4,600 million years, during which we have acted in accord with the conviction that nothing changes. Now, after a century of anachronous unconcern, we can anticipate crises apropos of excessive population and scarcity of water.

153

Man plans and lives his life on condition of constancy; and because nothing stays quite the same for even one second, to record matter in writing is to store it, the very action of which antiquates it.

154

We are on earth for no reason or cause that is not inherent in the merest weed.

155

Feedforward (as opposed to feedback) is the communication to the brain by receptor nerves of impending circumstances. Feedforward is a function that is essential for smooth and efficient physical and mental action. Because of feedforward, a hasty reader, vaguely registering only the general shape of words, will sometimes develop false memory of having read something he did not read.

156

Respectively, from concept to consummation, thought contains consciousness, feeling, imagery, and language. Consciousness is the stem cell of thought; that is, it is essential to all thought. Feeling, imagery, and language are the three consecutive steps leading to formulation of thought. Not that it happens with mechanical concision, but it happens.

157

All man's experience must be imagined, whether real experience or merely imagined experience; and all memories are the stuff of imagination, whether the remembered matter was real experience or merely imagined experience. The memory of real experience generally impresses the mind more deeply than imagined experience; nevertheless, because imagination is man's entire extent of intelligence, all remembered experience is in the broad category of imagined experience. Some distortion of memory will result therefore from false information and/or accidental relationships occurring among one's constellation of values and one's repertoire of remembered experiences.

158

What one learns is related by mental association to what one learns at about the same time, and the memory of one is likely to evoke the memory of the other, enhancing the creativity of analogy.

159

From the time votaries of any system have developed a loyalty to that system, that system's support is based on more than its merits and is judged without consideration of its usefulness. It is from that time liable to be maintained in spite of doing harm as well as good. The sentiments that support loyalty can accrue from length of obligation, on which loyalty grows like barnacles on a boat.

160

Addiction to overeating, as far as I know, has been battled only through the imagination; that is, by employing willpower. An aid to willpower can be mounted through the physical senses: taste, smell, and feeling. A very effective ally, for example, is a strong mouthwash. Gargled immediately after finishing a proper meal and before consuming the few extra bites, as usual, that cause weight gain, the refreshing sharpness of a strong mouthwash will nullify the eating mode in the brain by rendering the mouth and throat sensorially incompatible with eating.

161

Continuing to read after reading material that has been found very impressive is not conducive to efficient learning, because the brain is still reverberating with the impressive material it has just learned. To learn matter that is not impressive, we have to do the reverberating ourselves. We have to use multiple presentations and reviews.

162

In the Christian Bible, St. Matthew, Chapter 13, verses 3 through 8, Jesus, explaining that some sown seeds will be consumed by birds, some will fall on barren ground, but some will fall on fertile ground and do well, describes natural selection in function ages before Darwin's discovery of it.

163

Man is a born actor. Because his brain evolved as a monitor of external conditions, man cannot be himself. He can take control of himself only by effecting an external stimulation of himself which he obeys. This is the cause of the evolution of intracommunicative vocalization which man sends out, audibly or imaginatively, from his vocal faculties in the guise of his own expression and receives through his hearing faculties in the guise of information from an external source. Thus by self-instruction man assumes mastery over himself.

164

The two people that every single person is can be true comforting and encouraging friends to each other. Unlike "friends" who are different persons and therefore cannot truly communicate one with the other, the two persons who are the same person can truly communicate. With their conversation they can truly teach and learn from one another without the doubts and vagrant assumptions interfering that are an inevitable part of the interchange between separate persons. The evidence of this is simply that, in the interchange between separate people, the commonest characteristic is misunderstanding.

165

The principal factors in the generation of living matter are time and the infinite smallness, number, and variety of the particles that constitute matter, to which Gerald Edelman's concept of degenerate matter (redundancy of varied subatomic particles) is germane.

166

I believe natural selection is always progressive; for progress must necessarily be adaptation to the conditions that support life on the parent planet; and natural selection destroys all nonadaptive forms of life, allowing only adaptive forms to survive.

167

When one has adjusted oneself to a living condition, that condition of life is as tolerable as any other livable condition. If a person is imprisoned for a crime, for example, and fully adjusts to prison life, it will be just as traumatic for that person to be freed as it was for him or her to be imprisoned; for the brain works always to adjust to current conditions. If it were not for this function of adjustment, how could we have tolerated life under the conditions prevalent in the seventeenth and eighteenth century cities, with their thousands of citizens emptying their chamber pots out an upper window into the street every day? It's easy to understand from the literary productions of the time that the people were so adjusted to this custom that it excited little or no remark.

168

If metaphor is the use of one idea (a particular symbol) to denote another, then language is entirely metaphor. All words are metaphors: making certain sounds or symbols to bring to mind certain objects or conditions. The omnipresence of metaphor in intellectual life points to the importance of association in thought and memory.

169

Permanence is a fallacious human invention of the same type as psychic engulfment. Like psychic engulfment (the mistaken belief that one's world is everyone's world and that one's point of view is shared by all), permanence is assumed to exist because of appearance: the natural progression of change is too slow for immediate notice. Both these fallacious presumptions cause countless troublesome difficulties on all levels of society.

170

The human brain, in the resting state, makes two percent of the body's weight, uses fifteen percent of the body's blood and twenty percent of the body's oxygen. It must be possible to lose weight merely by thinking.

171

Man's principal survival faculty during his evolution was undoubtedly interpersonal cooperation, and social affinity is undoubtedly genetically programmed in the human psyche. A person, therefore, who is averse to all human society is not personally and socially normal. That person must sometime during his or her early development have had a formative social experience that was traumatic and pivotal.

172

When we read an absorbing novel, we dwell, in our most intense awareness, in the place and under the conditions in which the story is set. We identify with the protagonist and feel his guilt, anger, fear, and joy. For some time after we stop reading, we carry these feelings with us when minding our own affairs, living and learning, for a space, from two lives.

173

Two things that work against each other in our society are the fact that nothing stays the same and our presumption that everything stays the same. Our laws, customs, and our federal constitution are antiquated because the conditions for their use has changed.

174

It's the nature of reading to arrange meaning in the reader's mind first by feeling, then by imagery, and finally by language, this last being usually internalized and silent. The effect of the imagery is to give the reader an instant picture of the scene indicated. If a character in a story says, for example, "I walked into a small cafe," the reader at once pictures the tables and chairs, the table cloths and napkins. His will be a picture of the interior of a small cafe that is uniquely his; different than the picture in the mind of the author or of any other reader. The word "café" entails the reader's entire picture of the interior of a small cafe. The final formulation of thought is thus furnished by the author; but the reader furnishes the imagery and resolves the meaning and significance from his own life's experience. He or she is very much a cocreator of the final effect.

The reader responds to the printed word with a feeling, actually a tiny (but not always tiny) shock, as the meaning goes rapidly through feeling, image, and speech. The shock is the effect of the brain's sudden setting of the entire body of the reader in a mode to apprehend and react to a new meaning; which, depending on the involvement of the reader, is of a more or less agitating import. This exercise of the perceptive faculties is the more invigorating and the more thoroughly appreciated by the reader for the fact that it entails the motivated and deliberate mental action of the reader, who must create the imagery and grasp the meaning from mere words. The substance of the text is the more appreciated for being not only something conveyed, but also something earned.

175

Aleksandr Romanovich Luria (1902-19770, Soviet psychologist, experimented seven years to give scientific credence to the proposition that one cannot control one's own behavior by the power of one's own will; one can control one's own behavior only by indirect means. While one is concerned with the problem requiring action, one is paralyzed by its emotive urgencies. One must concern oneself with something that is free of the emotion and yet catalytic to the required action, something that serves as a catalyst to the action and is not involved in the conditions to be changed.

For example, this morning I applied Luria's postulation to my holding a warm compress on my closed eyes for at least five minutes. This was very hard for me. I got very impatient, feeling I was wasting time. So I started timing myself by counting off the small parts of time that I judged to be seconds. I counted to sixty five times. This made the waiting easy. It was controlling my behavior by indirect means. It was doing something. It kept my mind off my sense of urgency.

Twirling a hat to prevent its tumbling when tossing it onto a bed is analogous to controlling behavior by indirect means. Luria found speech, usually internalized and silent, to be the ideal activity by which the cultured human being indirectly controls his own behavior.

176

We see things in relation to what we expect. We are more impatient waiting four seconds for a computer to perform an operation than we used to be waiting thirty seconds for ink to dry when writing with a fountain pen. We feel more pressed for time with all our timesaving devices than we felt before we had them.

177

Expectation is projection into the future. It is prejudgment (prejudice). It is making extra use of relativity by seeing things in relation to what we expect as well as to what we know. As feedforward, it is much to our advantage.

178

Attention is like a spotlight that can flash over the experiences of an entire lifetime in a very few seconds; and many various preformed, enabling, and facilitating modes (that is, manners of functioning) lie quiescent in the brain awaiting arousal by attention. Attention activates existing modes and, in reaction to new experience, stimulates the development of new modes. While a mode is featured by attention, the parts of the brain that structure the mode work rapidly by strengthening some synapses (connections between neurons) and weakening others and by forming new synaptic routes to make the doing of whatever one is doing easier, more effective, more efficient, and therefore more enjoyable. The ability of attention to stimulate quiescent modes or the development of new modes depends on whether the attention is intent enough to trigger synaptic response. The modes most strongly energized are usually the modes most important for survival, eating and sexual intercourse. Circumstance, however, or, more importantly, one's resolution and fixity of purpose can cause most any mode to predominate, energized by our immediate interest. Knowing this about the brain, its modal activity, and the importance of attention management, can be of value to one in the management of one's life.

One's habitual way of eating, for example, a very important feature of one's lifestyle, is often in need of stricter control. During a meal one's attention is on eating; and the brain is mapping, remapping, and adjusting synaptic routes conducive to a greater enjoyment of this activity. By the end of a meal, one's brain is very much in the eating mode. At the end of a sufficient meal, in fact, one feels a stronger impulse to eat than at the beginning of the meal, when one is truly hungry. It's almost impossible, immediately after a meal, to refrain from taking one or two more bites of that enticing pie or cake, the very bit extra that puts on the weight; and the enticement is several times stronger for the fact that one's attention is on eating; which is to say one is *thinking* about eating, energizing an already-engaged mode.

This is the time to remember a fact of surpassing importance: *one's attention is under one's control.* If one forces one's attention onto a subject that has nothing to do with eating, one's brain will quickly switch to the task of making that new subject more interesting and enjoyable to think about and making it perhaps not easy, but several times easier to get away from the table. Even more effective in keeping the attention locked away from food would be starting to physically *do* something besides eating, as the physical action would more firmly anchor the attention. It helps, too, to decapacitate the taste buds by gargling a strong mouthwash when one wishes to stop eating.

Because learning is habit formation, if one does remain resolute and one does succeed in holding out for the time it takes the eating mode to become inactive, one will have established in one's brain a mode for defeating the desire to yield to the eating mode when one has eaten a sufficient amount; and when, after one's next meal, attention awakens that mode, it will be easier to prevail again, and still easier, after each success, to succeed again and again. This is because the abstaining mode will have improved and strengthened itself each time it receives the energizing effects of attention.

179

Feedforward in league with psychic engulfment is what makes one see one's handwriting as easily legible when others see it as illegible. This is because we see things as our expectations prepare us to see them (feedforward); and because we see everyone living in the same physical world, we thoughtlessly assume everyone lives likewise in the same mental world (psychic engulfment). This same illusion accounts for innumerable misconceptions in all walks of life.

180

Three things I can't believe of adult intelligence: (1) Jack London not thinking to eat snow when he was suffering acutely from thirst and wading in fresh snow, looking for a river (see his book *The Road*, pages 108-9); (2) "Porphry's Letter to His Wife Marcella" being mistaken for an account of his philosophy; and (3) Oscar Wilde's account of a lover's spat (his essay "De Profundus") being mistaken for a profundity.

181

Reading, pronouncing, and writing a word greatly aids the learning of that word. The reason is that the more of our different experiences we expose to any concept, the more effectively we learn that concept; that is, the longer we will remember it and the more circumstances we will recognize it under. This triple exercise impresses the word on three facets of our many-faceted experience.

182

Because evolutionary survival favored intelligence, natural selection made the brain to go through many reproductive cycles during the life of the body. This makes the brain grow faster than the cranium; and the gradual accretion of molecular pressure, like grass breaking concrete, can become uncontainable.

183

Nothing makes more sense than Hegel's dialectic materialism, in regard to which thinkers always make the mistake of applying it only to conditions they wish to see changed. The formula of thesis, antithesis, and synthesis works in regard to everything; and this includes the reign of the human species as predominant earthly beasts. The resistance man is accumulating against his continuing reign may be in many small increments, in one large unit, or in a combination of the two; but we may be sure it is building. Perhaps it will be overpopulation and consequent exhaustion of Earth's supply of water, or perhaps the technical shrinking of Earth will cause a too-general interface between opposing forces, together with the creation of world-destroying weaponry. There are many possibilities.

184

I think aromatherapy may have certain efficacies, because the smell of cedarwood and also of new leather make me nauseous. This proves smells can have a harmful effect on a physical organism. I assume, though it has never been proved to me, that smells can also have a beneficial effect.

185

We can make good use of the fact that we are the most imitative animal on earth. If we want to learn to do something, as it may be write a certain way, we need only read something written that way. We will then find it a bit easier to write that way due to our innate tendency to imitate.

186

Because survival was and is the sole propelling factor available to all entities during the evolution of life on earth, to escape destructive situations is the prevailing genius of every earthly entity; and because everything that exists, exists by virtue of surviving the ravages of nature, this applies to both organic and inorganic entities. Every earthly entity, therefore, has been especially styled by the ravages of nature for survival; and every cognitive creature is especially equipped thus by natural selection to become quickly aware of how forces and situations external to itself relate to each other and most importantly to itself. Our entire conception of existence, therefore, had to be built from this standpoint, of which relativity is the fundamental element. This is why all cognitive creatures on earth can think only relatively and why we can see anything for what it is, or indeed even see it at all, only by relating it to what it isn't, never by considering it by itself alone. It's the nature of inanimate objects also to resist change, because inertia evolved in an environment where development depended on escaping destruction.

187

The knowledge learned best by man is the knowledge a child acquires to assess the emotions of its parents. This knowledge is, for the child, the most germane to survival and is learned when little else distracts the mind.

188

Branching makes determinism indeterminate; because, by branching, one cause may have more than one effect, even many.

189

What does art do that gives it real value? I can think of seven functions of it.

(1) Art entertains.
(2) Art orients people to the experiences of nature and society.
(3) Art orients people to their culture.
(4) Art teaches, increases, and strengthens people's culture.
(5) Art modifies culture.
(6) Art in common household articles promotes contentment and serenity.
(7) Art affects man in his most important faculty, his mind.

190

When a warm object is pressed against one's flesh, it starts to cool. At the same time, one's flesh starts to warm. Soon their temperatures are the same. Thus nature tells us togetherness fosters tolerance.

191

Animals enjoy exercising their major forms at play that were acquired at anything but play. The rabbit enjoys exercising its faculty for speed; the bull plays at butting. Man, especially, has developed psychological and social modus operandi, not only for the avoidance of tragic situations, but also for the easing off of the emotional anguish he experienced during the centuries of tribal wars and sorcery. The major forms were made by natural selection like the conveyance worn in a stone by a steady fall of water, and the final form that evolved and reigns now in the time of war is the love of grief. In England during the time of the romantic poets they owned the love of melancholy; and now, in the USA, we deny that the tedium of everyday life makes a joy of grief that draws the love of one for all through the crustaceous shield of shame.

192

A clue to how long man has had language could be the location and degree of development of Broca's area of the brain, which controls talking, and of Wemicke's area, which functions in the understanding of speech.

193

The need to strive makes anticipation satisfying to us and makes tedium hard to bear. It makes us bored with what we strive to get: peace and contentment.

194

Words revise reality because we are born into a reality that is chaotic, and every earthly brain must construct for itself a world that makes enough sense for living in. Thought is formulated with words; so the world we build is built of words and is only roughly parallel to the chaos of reality. We exchange a real world of disorder for an artificial world of order. The "facts" we live by do not touch reality, but stay roughly parallel with it. They require constant revision.

195

The Watusi and Masai of the level African savanna are 6.5 to 8 feet tall. Both herd cattle. The Masai leap as high as they are able in dancing. They need the height to see enemies and beasts farther away. All the savanna dwellers are tall because of mating preference and because the short perished.

196

All the weird superstitions related to death practiced by primitive peoples, much of whose worlds were seen only in the imagination, as well as our own religions were exercises of the ability to split off from and deny reality. This was necessary for man during his evolution to make him capable of bearing up under the catastrophes that were common in his life. They amounted to a protective schizophrenia. This is the basis of the taboos that held the primitive world as in a social straitjacket. Man thus developed an ancient tolerance for tragedy and is genetically addicted to it.

197

The fact that an excellent and extensive brain would have survival value in adapting to and manipulating reality is an idea that man has accidentally become conscious of during the last three thousandth of one percent or less of his existence as a cognitive animal. Before that, the brain was used to help man emotionally to survive catastrophe by the concoction of superstitions, myths, religions—escape from reality; that is, social schizophrenia. Primitive man's every movement was prescribed by some god or demon.

198

The fact that no offspring is quite like either parent—the fact that makes evolution of species possible and inevitable—is due to that fortunate and ubiquitous condition, disorder, the secret of our existence as well, I suppose, as of the existence of the entire universe. It is through disorder that life finds a way to survive in almost any environment.

199

The many superstitions, which affect so much that a primitive people does, allow the people to avoid responsibility for the many tragedies that affect their lives. Magic spirits are to blame when someone dies or becomes ill. These shock absorbers must be used to satisfy the instinct for which they are safeguards—the instinct to emotionally survive catastrophe. Sometimes these superstitions, so valuable emotionally, are detrimental practically. For example, some primitive peoples have tabooed so many foods that they suffer from malnutrition.

200

The macho persuasion in television and other communication peculiar to our culture causes parents to train their infants to be so fearless of water and other dangers that many die, causing those who have a strong predisposition to be afraid of dangerous situations to survive oftener to produce offspring like themselves. This would affect the evolution of man, making him a more timid animal. Of course, this might be conducive to the survival of the species. Persuasion doesn't grow weaker the more it is passed on, but like a neuronal impulse at a synapse, it acts as a catalyst and picks up new energy from the persuaded. Thus, it may become stronger as it goes along.

201

Social workers have learned that some families need anxiety. Since they were raised in a state of anxiety, they need it in order to feel secure. This is a case of engrams (memory traces) getting so well implanted that they are a permanent form of the brain, a habit become instinct. Thus we are changed by environment.

202

Man's greatest invention was not the wheel; it was the lie. If he couldn't have imagined things as they were not, he couldn't have invented the wheel.

203

A vivid example of misconceived immutability is experienced on meeting an elderly man last seen or heard from as a childhood playmate.

204

The most overlooked fact in the world: after every act there is a reconsideration, resulting sometimes in approval, sometimes in disapproval of the act, or anything between; but the act makes a different and unpredictable impression in its done side than it made just prior to. This, like many a worse event, is a parameter of fallible function; and no intelligence or judgmental discretion can foretell the feeling that will follow the accomplished act.

205

When a dog kills a baby, it's because the baby has bothered the dog and does not know how to give the signs of submission which would inhibit attack, as a puppy would. It's well to remember that a dog thinks like a dog.

206

Everything known is conditioned by the knower, for every word used by any person has a unique signification for that person. It cannot be otherwise if experience affects different people differently, which it is known to do.

207

I have noticed people socializing, telling each other nothing more informative than "this is the kind of person I am." They do nothing more constructive than display themselves and explore each other. It is preoccupation with social play that has enabled man to live hundreds of thousands of years without discovering anything more materially useful than the stone ax and the frictional production of fire, though possessing a brain nearly equal to that of modem man.

Social play may not be constructive thinking, but it is very deep and agile thinking. It had a lot of influence in mate selection and also in survival, through bluff and cunning among enemies and rivals.

Man's brain needed a ready-made supply of puzzles to exercise on, and it had it in his fellow creatures. This exercise was crucial to his evolution in mate selection, in improving his chance of surviving by learning better how to hunt and fight, and as mental exercise in the mysteries of personal intercourse. Creative thought is a by-product that has now been discovered.

208

Our memory is based on association. Metaphor is based on association. We think with metaphor; that is, by association. Every word one uses is a metaphor; for there is a partial likeness to its referent that a word acquires, just as a person's name assumes that person's personality for his familiars; and it is this partial likeness that we exploit to refer metaphorically to the word's referent. Suppose, for example, in our everyday affairs, we need to be able to refer to the object we now call a desk. This object, however, has no name. It makes no appeal to any of our senses that is not made by many other objects, or we might call it the smooth, the beige, or some such name, according to its sensual stimulation. The fact is, we handle it mentally several times every day; so we must give it something to mentally handle it by, a mental handle. For any of several reasons, for no reason, or simply because we need a name for the object, we call it a desk. This name assumes thereafter a mental similarity to the desk by being its name. We associate the sound of the word desk with a mental image of the desk, by virtue of which we can now think of the desk metaphorically, which is the only way we can think about anything. We have to cross the chasm of differentness by association; and since we are different from everything but us, we have to do all our thinking by the use of metaphor.

There are several material neurotransmitters that carry information across synapses between neurons in the brain; but the only conceptual transmitter is association. One's intelligence depends partly on the sensitivity and orderliness of one's associative powers; and therefore the most rewarding study in all academia, as affording the most exercise to the associative powers, is simply reading. Reading anything, that is, at all. For words, but for the association we have arbitrarily given them, are but squiggles of nonsense. Reading, we rapidly associate words with referents of almost infinite variety, cementing the association of word and referent with imagery and language in passing.

209

If I were given the duty of finding the most important advice to give any person, regardless of age or sex, I would say, "Learn the meanings of words, for that is the key that opens the door to all knowledge."

210

If we bring to bear in our immediate awareness the undoubted fact that others take communication from us as new evidence concerning us to which our own thoughts and feelings have no relevance, and that our communicatee's thoughts and feelings, of which we are totally unaware and which are based on a background so alien to us as utterly to disorient our conception of him—that is to say if we could realize penetratingly what was actually passing in every encounter with any person, if we could eradicate all psychic engulfment and see the truth of the encounter, it would change our conception of the truth of the encounter in its entirety and leave us incredulous and wiser.

211

Strong evidence of feedforward (being informed of one's immediately impending circumstances) is the fact that, wondering if I had turned on the fan while I walked on my treadmill and not being able to turn and look, I held out my hands to see if I could feel the air from the fan. I expected to feel the air, because I thought I had turned on the fan. I truly felt a good strong current of air and so was satisfied that the fan was on. When I finished exercising, I discovered I had not turned on the fan, and the current of air I had felt was only an imaginary product of feedforward.

212

In a country with a free enterprise economy, to do someone a good turn is likely to make the good Samaritan one or more enemies. This is because in such an economy, the rule is that each must look after himself and his own dependents; and to do a good turn to one, unless the act is made appropriate through some conventional custom, is unsettling to the ethnic balance. To give someone unrequested money is contrary to common policy. The recipient thinks the donor a fool and himself unjustly pitied, and others think themselves slighted.

213

In the negotiating of international differences, the fact that the negotiators do not have to do the fighting in case of war has a great influence on the likelihood of compromise.

214

What's the effect of baby talk on the baby? Remember the baby is learning from this talk.

215

There's a social cancer that has been growing in American society for centuries: our failure to properly cultivate our youth. One of our many anachronous erroneous beliefs is the belief that a teacher's precepts and examples exposed briefly to a score or so of children every day can affect their characters.

216

We can't think in the abstract because we think with imagery, and images are concrete.

217

We can easily illustrate that we learn from what we know. If two children are being taught to spell the word *cat,* and only one of them has learned the alphabet, then only the one who has learned the alphabet will learn to spell the word *cat.*

218

Man objectifies his psyche by talking to himself, facilitating thought by creating a condition under which thought is held effortlessly in context.

219

Jost's law, that of two equal impressions the first experienced will be remembered longer, is true because the first entails the greater change.

220

Feedforward (being informed of impending conditions) guides us in every step we take walking down the street; we button our coat efficiently because of it; we learn more efficiently for its illuminative foresight. Walking in the park, we feel the terrain we tread before we take a step. Feedforward lets us enjoy the familiar. Its language spreads throughout the place where we live, house and neighborhood, and makes us love our home more the longer we live there. It doubles our enjoyment by giving us an experience once in anticipation and again in actuality.

221

"And" I have always thought to be a conjunction. Nowadays, however, it doubles as a disjunction, as in separating the last two of a series of discrete members. For example, "They hired a plasterer, a painter and a carpenter." To be clear, there must be a comma after "painter"; for one could mistake a painter and a carpenter as two parts of a discrete work team. Happily, language settles toward simplicity like the earth settles toward level. However, the laziness that inspires this fortunate realization should mind the requirements of meaning. Suppose a clothing merchant left a note for his employee as follows.

"You must bring red, white, brown and gold jackets as well as purple skirts."

The poor employee could ask himself, "Does he mean brown jackets and gold jackets or brown and gold jackets?"

222

The recipient of meaning through language must make his own estimate of its germinal formulation by his own feeling and its medial formulation by his own imagery and must give it a final formulation in speech according to his own conception of language before he can be said to grasp it. What he finally understands is of his own birthing, not the meaning proffered by his informant, but a cousin to it, thrice removed.

223

Evidence that words influence mental conception is in the simple fact that different people derive different concepts from the same word, for different people have had different formative experiences relevant to any word. There is further evidence in the fact that no two synonyms in one's native language evoke quite the same image in one's mind. The even simpler fact that words evoke conceptions according to the sounds of the words is sufficient evidence that every person's world is a unique construction built of one's words according as one understands and reacts to the uses of the words. Snake, serpent, and viper all evoke different images in my mind, as do nag, jade, and plug. Also squeezing and compressing, vendor and peddler, purse and wallet, traveler and wayfarer.

224

The partitivist (my term, meaning hair splitter) makes every concept an organization of many interdependent parts, each discrete from all the others, but each allegedly essential to the function of the whole. Each of the many discretely functional parts consists of several discretely functional parts, each of whose function allegedly must be separately explained in order to make sense of the whole. The entire production is coated finally with the modest concession that a really thorough and complete explanation of the least functional unit would fill a ponderous volume in small print, this to explain what might have been explained in one paragraph or simply taken for granted. All this gives the impression that those working with or teaching these concepts have lots of essential work to do.

225

An unexamined life is worth living because all is relative. Plato's statement that it is not worth living is only the way he feels about it; that is, it's a statement of Plato's private values. He gives no empirical reason or cause for his feeling. A person who wouldn't know how to examine a life might find his life well worth living; and he would be just as right as Plato.

226

Much of language is onomatopoeic. Read Tennyson's poetry to sense this. "Roar," "ring," "bell," "shove," "push," "hit," "scurry," "pour," and such like words sound like part of what they describe. Many words, however, were built of infixes from other words.

227

Counterpoint emphasizes poetic rhythm and rhyme by putting contrasting expressions in their place. It's analogous to underemphasis for greater effect, which is called meiosis (pronounced my-O-sus). It introduces a bit of awkwardness to accentuate the grace it displaces, as a dash of bitters will sharpen the taste of whiskey, a bit of ugliness enhance the beauty of a woman.

228

No water can be utterly hot if it can boil, and no person can be utterly lonely if he can talk to himself. He can imagine a conversant.

229

The fact that thought is feeling is not entirely commensurate with the scientific method; it allows the deviation of too much belief due to desire alone. It makes much training necessary for the scientist.

230

The force that guides the world's ways is not in the hands of man. Man strives to change the world's ways through literature, politics, and religion; but each person in the world is unique, and the vast conglomeration of their differences gives the world a guidance beyond the control of man. The need is to get all or nearly all of the people to work toward a single goal. Politics appears sometimes to be partly successful; and literature, in a longer time frame, has some effect. Religion has had a merely nominal effect, for the main concern of its adherents, as of all the citizenry, has always been money (see *The Illustrated Chronicles of Matthew Paris*). These variant forces move the world in a sometimes predictable, but never in a controllable direction. History and sociology are two studies germane to this problem.

231

Animals probably formulate and anchor their thoughts with mere sounds, sounds unstudied and only roughly and unconsciously regulated according to meaning. Their language being for the most part private, the meaning of a sound need be remembered only until its immediate use; a different sound might be used for the same meaning each time it is used. The same sound might be used for every meaning; but some anchor of meaning they must employ to hold thought until it can be used, if they think. And that animals think is beyond dispute.

232

When we act in the interest of survival, we are not thinking of genes. The body and its reaction to environmental conditions are our concerns. It's the body that is exposed to the environment, and it's the body that must take care of the business of survival. The body changes to accommodate necessities imposed by environmental conditions, and the genes change to accommodate the necessities imposed by the body. The genes carry the blueprints for the body, but the body draws the blueprints.

233

Our keeping an alleged felon in jail a length of time before his trial is an injustice, for the suspect is innocent until proven guilty. We should have a "holding only" kind of detention, very comfortable, to hold the suspect until we determine his or her guilt or innocence. Also, the suspect's family should be allowed to visit or live with him or her during this provisional detention.

234

Mythology is an artificial representation of reality, not true, but understandable. It allows man to believe he understands reality. All man's knowledge is mythology, his conception of reality. He cannot take reality in without distorting it by his cognitive processes, biased by his past experience. He can take only such impressions of it as articulate the mythic world in which he lives.

235

If a person makes a declaration and then enumerates several items of evidence in support of his declaration, one or more uncalled for, one should be alert for an ulteriorly based motive in that person instrumental to his material or emotional advantage.

236

We often fail to enjoy a book because it is not what we expected it to be; when, had we no expectations of it, we would have enjoyed it well enough. People don't like to be surprised; they like their anticipations to be prescient. They are ready to appreciate the expected, and it would mean building a whole new mental construct to get ready to appreciate something different.

237

Variation is not just the spice of life; it's the essence of life. We can't see things move, for there has to be contrast for us to see or hear at all. Our eyes show us still pictures, more than a thousand per second. Sense lag joins them together, and we think we see things move. We can't hear prolonged sounds. We hear frequent sound waves, sense lag joins them, and we think we hear tones. The changes are from sight to no sight to sight, from sound to no sound to sound. The same with smell, taste, and touch. Our lives are filled with change, night and day, sleep and waking, hunger and repletion, thirst and quenching of thirst, youth and age, happiness and despair. We can't abide constancy.

Sense lag brings our separate sensations together and gives us memory. Without memory, we could have no mind; without mind, we could not live. Constancy of any kind is a violation of nature. Marriage is not a natural institution; from the very vows that join, we begin to resent the marital restrictions. All discipline is a distortion of nature; diligence runs counter to it; steady work is a natural absurdity; behavioral control is impossible without an immediate goal in view. A goal is made immediate by language. Nature is distorted in the coils of speech. Our lives are formulated with words. Language makes life an illusion and we strive for the illusory goals it makes appear before us. We live by self-deception, and but for silent words of self deceit, would still exist in roving tribes, a brother to the ape.

238

A man who is getting past the working age sees retirement as it compares with his working life, with the unpleasant experiences and time restrictions of employment. He sees retirement in relation to the freedom to do as he pleases, his time restricted only by the sun. After retirement, as he gets used to his total freedom, the trip by recreational vehicle around the United States that he had so long anticipated by comparison with the daily drudgery of his job begins to look like a long durance of danger, road rage, and fatigue—no longer an exercise of freedom, but a long and laborious, self-imposed vexation. A hundred miles down the highway, he turns around and comes home, puts the RV up on blocks in the front yard, pours himself a highball, and brings a lawn chair out under the shade tree.

239

During World War One the government of France and Germany supplied each other strategic war materials with the object of keeping the astronomically profitable conflict in progress, committing, thereby, mass murder for money on a mastodonic scale (See *Days of Our Years*, by Pierre van Paassen, pages seventy through seventy-seven). The conflict was also astronomically destructive of human life; for thousands were dying every day in the muddy, blood-soaked trenches between France and Germany. Soldiers were becoming scarce; it became necessary to conscript mere boys and old men. Still dreading loss of the unprecedented wealth they were reaping by their contraband commerce, they managed to reject every proffered plan to end the war.

Reading of this unthinkable crime, I realized no common construct of crime and punishment could encompass its dreadful iniquity. If the murder of one man for money would get a murderer twenty years in prison, punishment would not answer here. These ultramurderers were of the class accustomed to administer punishment to others. They were respected in their communities; no type of punishment would reform these decent and honest citizens. They were as good as people get. If the miserable deaths of tens of thousands of innocent victims did not wake remorseful sympathy in these killers, then remorse was not there to wake. Their inconceivable crime had to be due, not to evil intent, but to a gap in the genetic makeup of humankind. However, by a reactionary transformation, later evolution of humanity engulfed this lacuna and made it indispensible to the survival of human life.

Those satiate on the profits of war, in control of tremendous wealth (which transmutes to power), are accommodated by a militant ideology fostered by interest in competitive sports in which victory is achieved by physical violence (e.g.: football, soccer, ice hockey). Such national attitude assures an automatic pro-combat stance toward international dissidence, which, as everyone knows, is certain, sooner or later, to occur. The effect of militant propaganda on such a public mind-set gets a ready reaction; war is approved, effecting the death sentence of innocent thousands and the impoverishment of all except the profiteers, a grotesque slaughter which might have been avoided by half the polemic discussion expended on the adoption of a county's disputed budget.

The part of human genetic structure purged by natural selection in the ubiquitous insufficiency here under discussion was the part essential to man's assessment of himself, the part that allowed self-consciousness, daydreaming, introversion. It was also the part that allowed one's imagination to focus on sympathy for others who were not related or in any way close to one. Its destruction was effected by disuse, for the dangers to which all animal life was subject during its early evolution were so imminent and so destructive that any creature that let its attention stray from exterior conditions was soon killed and eaten. The millions of years that encompassed man's early evolution were plenty of time for mutants due to genetic recombination to appear who lacked the genes necessary for this introspective behavior, and these fortunate mutants began a new, self-concerned, unfeeling variety of the human species. Adaptation to this modified genetic ensemble entailed a sharp increase in disagreements between individuals, such that every critical problem impacting society drew a plurality of options for solution, greatly increasing the chances of finding a successful one and without which the human species would not have survived to the present day.

Virtue is an invention of man alien to his inescapable animality; personal advantage is his ultimate impulsion. It might sanctify him somewhat to try to endow him, a la Kant, with a sense of duty by ubiquitous placarding and constant broadcasting of purificatory petitioning, as is allegedly done to advantage in Japan.

To hope natural selection will integrate genes for empathic sympathy is vain; for that would entail the attempt to insert manufactured genes for empathy, a favorable premarital mortality, or a favorably biased mate selection; and the unfeeling would probably have more money and thus the marital advantage.

240

The use of an adverb often suggests the anticipation of argument and thereby weakens the assertion it is meant to strengthen. Adverbs are properly used to distinguish what kind when there is more than one kind and to distinguish how much when that is important; for instance, "mainly" when it is important to show "not entirely."

241

The traits that help us survive mature at uneven rates; and some that mature late are functionally related to those already functional and stimulate those already functional traits to further development. Ethos, for example, having developed early with the acquirement of language, was further developed by the later development of agency, giving us someone to blame; in consequence of which our sense of right and wrong (our ethos) inspired us to establish the institution of war; and we determined to make things right by lethal force. The first war to end all war was fought with sticks and stones.

242

Human intelligence acquired its first and most effective developmental exercise in the study of the private worlds of other people, their thoughts, motives, and general personalities, all of which make an insoluble mystery to every person. Because no one is able either to penetrate another's private world or to reveal his own, the mystery that surrounds every individual is an exercise device that has so strengthened human intelligence as to enable it to create not only the primitive conventional belief that every stroke of good or bad luck is effected by an agent, but also has enabled it to such modem achievements as interplanetary travel and nuclear weaponry.

243

The immense cultural lag that separates humanity's few intelligentsia from its uncultured masses spells doom for the human species. We are unable to get united action on population control or on greed for wealth and power. The opposition factor is both necessary for survival (it renders us an essential source of alternate opinions) and fatal to life (it engenders war). We lack a certain type of wisdom. We believe what we want to believe; we believe things will take care of themselves. The average human intelligence cannot protect us from our acquirements.

244

The opposition factor is necessary but fatal (it gives us indispensable alternate opinions and fatal conflict); ethos works toward peace and causes war (it gives us righteous outrage); agency gives ethos a necessary component of war (it gives us someone to blame); democracy allows the corruption of culture (with free enterprise, it allows the uncultured to lead the cultured.) If man has descended from the ape, he hasn't descended very far.

245

The ancient stoics' denial of pain for a virtuous person is an example of maintaining a belief in the face of contrary evidence, an example of our ability to believe anything. If some of the world's most intelligent people (Xeno, Seneca, and many other stoics) can believe they are above the effects of pain and fear in spite of writhing in agony and blanching with fear, as the stoics were reportedly seen often to do, then a theory could never be dislodged by logical argument.

246

In the beginning a kind of substance fomented in the slime on the shores of oceans, lakes, and ponds that reacted sensitively to association of any kind with such affecting entities as light, odors, touch, vibration of the air, etc. This fomented substance, gradually, over eons of time, was transduced by stimulation of earthly elements into creatures with such vague forms as the hagfish and has, by natural selection, assumed the higher forms of life. We know there was such a substance and such forms; for our eyes react to light, our ears to vibration of air, our olfactory faculties to odor, etc.; and we know that anything that can happen, *given enough time, will* happen and if conducive to adaptation, its effects will remain. The animal sensorium, consisting of sensitive and retentive reception units built up over eons of time by natural selection, associates a certain sensation with an entity in its environment and determines that this sensation is essentially this entity. This acquisition of entities eventually occurs in regard to the animal's entire environment. Thus, the animal, by the use of its senses, determines its world. The animal creates its own unique world, and its retentive receptors retain its conceptions of its world more or less permanently by association. This is a practical and understandable way in which animals might manage to interact with their environment.

247

If reality were subjective; that is, if reality were whatever one imagined it to be (see Herbert Read, *The Innocent Eye,* page 8), this would tell us why no philosopher could ever agree with any other philosopher. It would also eradicate the basis from which philosophers operate (the generality of reality). It's not reality that's subjective. All men's conceptions of reality are too much alike for that. It's man's interpretation of reality that is subjective.

248

The areas of the brain that accommodate speech comprehension and silent speech and are used for thought and self-control are located low in the brain and are much grown over by other parts, indicating to me that man's understanding and silent speech date from early in his evolution. This early understanding consisted mainly of extended thought (thought carried by mental images, each of which is a consequence of the prior image and a cause of the following image), and required the holding in the mind of concepts embedded in imagery long enough for the thinker to consider their relation to germane concepts and conditions. To ballast this weightless cargo, sound is the only practical agent; and because the nervous system can respond only to change, sound is useful only if broken into serviceable bits of various sizes and shapes. It was thus that language was born. In the throes of the first efforts to think, the subconscious implementation of variable sound gave birth to language in its most important use, private and unique in every individual, understood by its user alone, and used silently and without awareness, the thinker being conscious only of the thought it formulated. Thought is a compact of feeling, imagery, and language, which last is the use of sound to formulate the imagery. This private language is the only one that is inherited in its complete form, for its morphology and syntax are determined automatically by the sequence of the action that stimulates its creation. This first manifestation of a private language takes place with the infant's first attempts to formulate an account of what is happening to it.

The part of the brain that accommodates audible speech, unlike that used in thought, is used for communication between persons and is located in the motor area at the very top of the brain. To communicate interpersonally, then, with more than threatening looks, blows, and bestial grunts, must be among the last of man's evolutionary achievements. Audible speech heralded a language common to an entire community, a language spoken consciously and created bit by bit over millennia of interpersonal association. It evolved into an invaluable vehicle of communication, a way to impress others with one's intelligence and personality, and a new attraction for display in the mating game. It also aids in the exercise of a function essential to the survival of the human species; namely, it facilitates disagreement among members of human society. Opposing opinions are based on diversity of formative experience and result in a diversity of solutions proposed for every critical problem facing a nation or tribe. If society acquiesced to the decisions of only one man or one like-minded group, it would soon fall prey to the mistakes due to the overexertion of such a singular bias.

The basic essence of thought is feeling; and to render it understandable, it is formulated first by imagery and then by language. If it is meant for interpersonal communication, it is further formulated by language to facilitate its understanding by the person to whom it is addressed. These formulary alterations falsify all thinking to a certain degree. Furthermore, the communicatee can receive this thrice-formulated thought through only his own unique mental structure which is constituted by his individual formative experiences. He reacts to it with feeling, which he formulates first with imagery and then with language, making the alterations five instead of three.

By its linguistic formulation, therefore, reality is made an effect of man; and in this sense Immanuel Kant's thing in itself is indeed inaccessible to any person. More importantly, man's artificial reality, like his source of contention, is essential to his continued existence on Earth; for to exist on this ever-changing planet, man must be infinitely adaptable. To be infinitely adaptable, he must be able to believe literally anything; and to have the strength of his convictions, he must be able to believe it with unregenerate pertinacity. His plural formulations that separate him from things as they are makes fantasy of his intellect and make-believe of his strongest convictions.

249

We love democracy, but require a single unit of government as final authority. The body, ruled by the brain, has served as model for all governments.

250

We do not control the economy; quite the reverse. The concern about money constricts the actions of our citizens and gives stability to society.

251

Mode has influence on our opinions and plans; and mode is vagile.

252

We are like a tree. A tree lives by its roots. Analogously, we live by our roots, which are our ancestral genes and our past experiences. All our present experiences relate somehow to the roots that consist of our genes and our past experiences. Our past experiences color all our experiences, all our thoughts, and all our emotions. Especially when we are old, they enrich our present experiences.

253

We write of old age as society sees it, not as it is essentially. The old are rich in experience. We forget.

254

Spoken words come and go; print stays. Moving pictures curtail thought, for we think in rapidly changing mental images. The book will ever be the treasury of knowledge for man. Print has caught the word at the instant of the delivery of its information and holds it for an infinitude of time at the moment of giving birth to its meaning.

255

If one's life becomes less eventful, the lesser events will soon move one as much as the greater events once did. This is a corollary of the inability to consider anything other than relatively, a condition manifest in all mentalities that have evolved under earthly conditions. It's also a corollary of the law of concentric reduction as well as a genetically-based protection from emotional disruption due to loss of self-respect on retirement in old age.

256

When one person serves many, he soon, because of his superior knowledge in his area of expertise, begins to feel superior to those he serves. It is only a very superior person who will or can avoid showing this feeling in several ways. This very human failing, so easy to tolerate in a waitress, can be a very serious problem in a bureaucracy serving a social need, where a feeling of resentment can preclude the object aimed at.

257

The Law of Concentric Reduction could more aptly be called the Law of Proportionate Reduction. When extended to psychology, the factors that stay in proportion are categories of feeling, as when an employer's worst worker quits or is discharged, the next worst worker, who was before considered not especially unsatisfactory, is now considered very unsatisfactory. An important corollary of this is the comforting thought that if we lose part of our income and have to live less extravagantly, we will, after a brief and automatic adjustment, be as happy as before.

Some of the categories of feeling are things that make us happy, things that make us unhappy, things that cause us to be anxious, things that interest us, things that make us proud, things we enjoy eating, things we consider to be beautiful, things we are ambitious to achieve, etc.

258

A tree must grow from its roots; a person must prosper according to how he prepared himself.

259

Rabindranath Tagore has said that a beautiful thing should not be displayed together with other beautiful things, as this would depreciate the artistic appeal of the entire number (see "A Japanese Garden," in *A Tagore Reader*). However, he did not say why this is true. Tagore's statement is true; and the reason is that, as tomographic experiment has shown, by altering synaptic routes and intensities of neurotransmission, one's brain adapts instantly to whatever one is doing, making that activity progressively easier, more efficient, and therefore more enjoyable. Thus, when one observes an interesting and beautiful painting, one's brain forms at once a mental construct contoured to the features of that particular painting, making that painting progressively more easily and efficiently appreciated and more enjoyable to observe. If another painting, however interesting and beautiful, is displayed in the proximity of this painting, the formulated mental construct contoured to accommodate the features of either painting will not fit the features of the other; and to the extent that both paintings share the observer's attention, both paintings will be deprived of the profound appreciation either would have inspired if appraised singly.

I suggest an experiment in which a few paintings be displayed singly, each in a small compartment of its own, quite closed off from all the others.

260

When you live alone, you can see yourself always in any chosen relation to everyone else. Or you can be unaffected by your relation to others. This leaves your mind free to act. When you are with someone, you have always in your mind your idea of how that person sees you. If you are old, you suppose she or he sees you as an old person. You can never escape the feeling of being old. If you are crippled, you are constantly aware of the supposed image of crippledness the other must associate with you. Living in unfavorable contrast with others is loneliness. Living alone, on the other hand, you are made aware of solitude only by taking thought. You are in the company of yourself. You don't feel alone; you feel only unhampered by the presence of anyone else. You can see yourself as you are without comparison or critique. You can accept yourself.

261

If the brain wishes to be free of responsibility to the body and live in a purely intellectual world of its own, it will do so in dreams. It does.

262

One can never "get into" another's world. One can affect the world of another, but only indirectly. Society, for example, has always expected to make a criminal acquiescent and cooperative by punishing him, taking it as granted that we all live in the same world. The effect society wanted punishment to have it believed would be understood and reacted to properly by the criminal. Instead, and never more than when he pretends to be docile, repentant, and reformed, the criminal sees the law as only a stupidly obverse opinion, as something he must manage his business in spite of. Also, in the inadequately socialized, punishment causes resentment and only strengthens his adverseness.

To combat crime more effectively, we must be aware of the indirect effects of our actions on others. I am reminded of the fable of the wind and the sun competing to make a traveler take off his coat. The fierce wind only caused the man to draw his coat closer about him. The gentle sun warmed the traveler and caused him to take off the coat. The wind was as those who assume we all live in the same world. The wind tried to make the man remove his coat by direct action; the sun performed an action that had the indirect effect on the man's world which made him desire to remove his coat. The implication is that we should so treat the criminal as to make him comply of his own will. The evidence of hundreds of years indicates he will not comply of anyone else's will.

263

The fact that we are genetically programmed for both unhappiness and happiness in any environment is a corollary of the fact that all things are relative. The environment will cause us to be unhappy or happy to a degree, but we are programmed to react according to what we are used to and what we expect; that is, to react relatively. All things have to be relative in order for anything to be known. If all things were not relative, nothing would be perceivable. Therefore, all things are relative that we know anything about.

264

Nothing we know about travels as fast as light; however, the speed of light is not absolute; that is, relative to nothing, because it is measurable. The speed of light is fastest relative to anything else. The suffix *-est* indicates as much.

265

Many say books give us many good things the screen does not give us and that, nevertheless, the screen will crowd the book out of its place in society. It is not so. All the screen will do is cause more people to appreciate reading, and these people will develop a taste for the beautiful use of words. It is said style in writing will go out when writing is done on-screen (E-mail). Again, no. E-mail, exposed on-screen for all to see, will inspire people with a desire to write better, and a taste for beauty in writing will cause people to appreciate books.

266

To do what a novel is supposed to do (broaden and deepen the experience of the reader), a novel doesn't have to be perfectly realistic; for the mind sees situations under variant conditions and employs analogy. The important thing is not that the novel teach the reader how to behave in a certain type of situation, but that it give him the vicarious experience of being in that type of situation. To do this it need be only plausibly realistic. The reader will get the experience of being in that type of situation and will learn from that experience his way or a better way to behave in it. The responsibility of the author is to tell the story so as to transport the reader to the time, place, and event, and to vivify them for him; that is, to practice his art.

267

We judge a person by the ritualistic frame he has built around himself in response to his upbringing, his social experience, and his weaknesses and strengths. This frame of rituals may be mediocre; but their interaction with reality within and concealed by this framework, which is his private world, may be exceptional.

268

Associating something with a vividly conceived image can help us remember it. The image is even more effective if we attempt to draw it.

269

The way advertising works: if you get the prospective customer to listen, he will experience the appealing aspects of your product in spite of himself. This will make a vestige of a habit in his way of thinking, very small, but a vestige.

270

What makes school a burden is not knowing how we are going to learn something. We are told to learn something and don't know how it can be done. This scares us. We must realize learning is simply forming habits. This is done by doing or thinking things repeatedly. This takes the mystery out of learning.

271

We transmit our attention so readily and so often from word to referent when using very common symbols, such as the word "house" or "road" in the final formulation of thought that our tolerance of the use of these words reaches the point of addiction and our attention simply fails to note them and focuses instead on the thought they formulate, rendering these common symbols units of what linguists call "internalized language," which is what we use silently and subconsciously in the process of thinking.

272

A culture based on superiority of the violent is insinuated in fiction generally and most effectively in movies shown in a darkened theater. Also in the popularization of violent sports. This in addition to saturation by ethnocentric patriotism keeps a nation ready to go to war. Are we just apes?

273

Alone in a strange city, features and details that you wouldn't notice if you had friends to distract you take on an emotional significance for you. And since you have no relation to them, their emotional significance, because it could be any kind, can be of multiple kinds at the same time. This is what Wolfgang Iser *(The Act of Reading)* thinks to be achieved by obscurity in the new fiction, exemplified by the work of Henry James. The function is the same as we experience in cartoon characters. We mentally finish the only half delineated portrayal, carrying the suggested characteristics to the extent we find appropriate.

274

To view a good painting with undisturbed concentration, taking time to potentiate the salience of its
principle genius and bask in its effect, would, I believe,
exceed imagery as alternative therapy (having the
patient imagine a consoling situation). Imagery has
proved its efficacy tomographically at reducing stress
and heart rate, stimulating the production of immune
cells, and, in elderly patients, at stimulating the production of killer T-cells. It has also helped patients endure
chemotherapy and arthritis and to prepare for sur-
gery. I believe deep study of a good painting treating
a consolatory theme, though identical to imagery in
technique, would have the advantage over imagery by
virtue of greater vividness of affect and greater stability
of attention.

275

One cannot consciously feel without thinking,
either by touching with the skin or by the body's reaction to a mental conception, for thought is feeling.

276

Mind is the function of the brain; it's neither a
condition nor a substance; it's an action.

277

The reason we see cartoon characters as being realistic is that their features are only partly delineated. We are allowed the freedom to assume the rest; and so our image of them is not restricted to only one likeness, but can be made according to our preference. It's like imagining the appearance of the author of a book from what he has written. We can entertain more than one mental image of a cartoon character and use either or any according to our mood. This principle is operative in viewing impressionist paintings, also. It complies, too, with the Zen and Taoist concept that true beauty is what the viewer finishes (mentally) to his own taste.

278

The consequences of conditions are all of equal significance as far as nature is concerned; the extinction of a species is quite as natural as its survival.

279

We have a fault of allowing a feeling to encroach on territory to which it has no relation and in which it has no meaning. An example is our disdain of the accomplishments of citizens of a country with which we have been at war. This prevents a great harvest of knowledge.

280

Ignorance is a defect that is responsible for much happiness. For the young it's a substrate for an enticing mystery that enables them to picture the unknown as whatever they wish it to be and allows them to approach the unknown with happy anticipation. The person who remains ignorant all his life of all except the knowledge necessary in his own little contented niche feels himself always surrounded by an interesting rich and golden never-never land of whatever kind he cares to imagine; and if the educated could not look to the unknown for further conquest, they would be bored.

281

Many high achievers owe their success to a challenge incited by a defect.

282

Citizens on the dole are of value to society, for they necessitate the distribution of money by the government to them, which they will necessarily spend. Because, in order to live, he must spend the money allowed him, each recipient of welfare is a small and efficient generator of prosperity.

283

The brain is an extra-sensitive, extra-retentive feeler, and thought is emotional reaction to mental—and, sporadically, to visual—imagery. Thought is thus feeling; and because words carry thought, the use of words is, of all his faculties, the closest to the mind of man. For this reason, an unusual use or pronunciation of a word can arouse a seemingly disproportionate rage in the heart of a communicatee. For this reason, too, reading, writing, and speech are the most important studies for the thorough cultivation of man.

284

You don't have to recall the exact word of a familiar language in order to think about the concept it signifies. The word will control the thought from the subconscious. Not being able to think of the name of a certain substance, you say, "That stuff"; and "stuff," for the purpose of thought, is just as good as the technical name; for you, the communicator, know what you, who in the act of thinking are also the communicatee, mean by "stuff" in that context. So the private language of an animal or a human infant would be very different than the common language. The private language, which needs to be understood by only its user, can take advantage of context, tone of voice, volume and whatever else can differentiate a word in the mind of its user. Even in the English common language there are many words that are identically spelled and pronounced, but have different meanings due simply to being used in a different context. For example, "spell," in "I can spell Mississippi" and "I will rest for a spell."

285

Thought is feeling; and, deny it as we may, we cannot keep our personal feelings unperturbed when challenged on an issue about which we feel strongly. It is not will power, therefore, that will keep one's emotions free and sublime and one's judgment in balance, but the undisturbing quality of the issue that occupies one's mind. A formula, beautiful in its simplicity, will help us maintain sublimity. When we feel our emotions beginning to unbalance our judgment, we should remind ourselves that one's opinions are fixed by one's experiences and that, given the same experiences, we, ourselves, would hold the opinion held now by our adversary. By this sensible circumspection we will be better able to keep a sedate demeanor in trying to introduce our adversary to the experiences that have made us feel as we do.

286

Wilhelm von Humboldt (1767-1835) conceived that the inherited human propensity to learn language molds vocal sounds into symbolic references to concepts, that is, into words, and that words formulate thoughts, which manifest by imagery and stimulate the brain to qualify and guide further thoughts. A.R. Luria (1902-1977) proved by extensive experimentation that one cannot think effectively without indirect stimulation of the brain by language. By the work of these two authorities, it becomes apparent that the brain, by reacting to its own linguistic concoctions, controls itself. Further, it is apparent that every creature that thinks through a sequence of images must control its thought by use of a private language that evolved subconsciously in response to that creature's needs and that is used subconsciously in the process of that creature's self-control.

287

Light doesn't come just to us from a star; it goes *all* ways from the star.

288

It is crucial to the improvement of human society that everyone lives in his own private and unique world, for this constitutes a cultural disconnect that enables the offspring to be different than either of its parents. The kind of parent a child will most willingly emulate is a kind and loving parent, and the kind and loving parent is a better citizen than an abusive parent. The inaccessibility of every person's private world allows the bad parent's child surreptitiously to build for himself an intellectual foundation to support a more enlightened future than that of his depraved parent, changing the direction of cultural progression from bad to better; so the human race is always improving ethically. Our average great grandchild will be better than the average person of today.

289

Our society can condone the putting to death of a criminal only if that is the only way to be sure so vicious and irredeemable a person will never again commit another such crime as the one for which he is condemned. Death must not be revenge, for that would divert juridical motives from justice. However, the death sentence must not be given if, when he committed the crime, the criminal was insane or so emotionally impaired that he could not control his actions; for then he could not be blamed.

290

People who claim animals think are right, but they thoughtlessly endow the animals with man's cultural background. In this, they are mistaken.

291

If the Bible were considered a fabular aid in teaching guiding principles of conduct to an ancient people who were too simple to understand the more abstract expressions necessary in a more direct teaching method, then religion might, by thus getting rid of its supernatural mythology, achieve that commensurability with science it has always tried to attain and might regain the respect its mythological version once commanded from a simpler population.

It is not unlikely that this was indeed the cause of so many occurrences described in the Bible that are impossible to believe to have been literally true. The confusion resulting in their being taken as literal truth could easily have infiltrated due to the impossibility of perfect understanding and the frequent incursions of gross misunderstanding that are present now and that were probably more pervasive when the Bible was conceived. Even more confusing must have been its countless translations into different languages.

292

Racial bias is a genetically based behavior trait acquired through the natural exercise of self-interest during the evolution of life forms. It is present in all extant cognizant creatures because those that lacked it suffered extinction. It dwells in the human subconscious like the roots of a tenacious weed that are ever ready to send forth new growth, though every vestige has been cut off above ground. To deal with its social consequences we must first concede this. Instead, because this fact has been stigmatized by propaganda, we deny it.

293

An experience lodged in the memory is rehearsed many times and each time by a mind transformed by increased familiarity; and so the memory evolves as the mind matures, each changing each.

294

Play involves extended thought, for it is imagined sequences of situations. Many animals play. Human infants play before they can use the common language. By this, we know they have devised, by the formula of an innate capacity, a private, internalized language; for words are necessary for extended thought. We think with images, and images change with every nuance of meaning. Words are the tools with which we control images for the formulation and direction of thought. "If you can't say it," it might legitimately be said, "you can't think it."

295

The background against which a concept is conceived has the greatest consequence for the feeling evoked by a work of art. By background, I mean not merely the immediate circumstances, but the permanent background, such as the horse-and-buggy days as opposed to the days of advanced technology. The squish of a horse's hooves in a muddy road, the squeak of the saddle as one mounted his horse—these had a different emotional effect then, than they would have in our time. Tennyson's poetry made a different impression when it was written than it makes today, in 2009. It was altogether different poetry then.

296

Intuition is the estimation of probabilities suggested by conscious and half-conscious associations.

297

Whenever a bureaucracy gets a procedure in place, its members, occupied with the problems of applying it, cease to see its advantages and notice only its shortcomings. So this first procedure has not long to reign before it is replaced by a second, which is soon to be jettisoned down the same chute in deference to the first, whose merits again look large by contrast with the frustrations of the second, whose good points will be once more prominent when the bureau has had another go at the first. Paying people to do this circulates the wealth and thereby helps to keep the economy healthy.

298

The games of curling and shuffleboard are good training in wisdom. They fundamentally teach one to balance force and moderation in everything one does.

299

No person can be taught; he can only learn. Only he can put knowledge and understanding in his own mind, for the knowledge and understanding has to find a proper niche in his constellation of values. It has to find a place to lie on his individual mental terrain, and none but he can find a place for it. An effective teacher is one who enables or causes her students to want to learn.

300

To do what it purports to do (that is, to get at truth), debate would have to be conducted like a game of chess, each participant being allowed up to several hours or even days to respond to a comment. It could best be carried on by letter. For one to respond to a statement with what he knows, what he can learn, and what he believes, he needs time to consider, to remember facts he may temporarily have forgotten, perhaps to look up matter to determine or confirm an opinion, perhaps even to debate a contingent issue. This would take time, and popular values do not rate truth so high.

301

Plants, I believe, are below consciousness. Or perhaps above it. Though some plants have what approximate nerves, they do not have anything that appears to be a brain. And they prove by their self-protection that self-protection can be genetically programmed by natural selection. Lacking any semblance of a brain, it is indisputable that the rose did not acquire its protective thorns through intellection. The Venus flytrap did not learn how to catch flies. The fir tree did not develop by invention the needles that make rain of fog.

All these protective devices are innate; none are learned; so we know some characteristics can be developed genetically; and since we have all had the experience of learning, we know some faculties can be acquired by learning, or by both learning and inheritance. No reason has ever been forwarded to show a characteristic cannot be partly innate and partly learned. Cooperative hunting among African lions and lodge building among beavers could be both innate and learned. Perhaps these animals have inherited a great aptitude for learning these strategies and skills and have learned them very well. This is the more likely in that some animals obviously and undeniably learn from other animals. Man, too, has a great aptitude for learning many things; for the learning of speech, for example, our natural aptitude is indisputable; some human infants learn to read before they learn to talk. But this precocious accomplishment is not entirely innate; the infant learns it from being read to; and most of us learn to read only after years of study.

302

What we call natural selection should have been called conditional consequence, for natural selection makes no needed adjustments in the process of evolution, and it doesn't destroy phenomena that are vitally incompliant with earthly conditions. It also makes no selections. These developments are not selected. They happen consequent to certain conditions.

The term "natural selection" causes even scientists to think of it as a discriminating agent in charge of evolution; for words, being the final formulators of thought, are the most influential stimulators of the mind. This conception of natural selection, therefore, often verbalized, will present as an omniscient controller.

Such misnaming allows too much intention in the conditions that advance evolution. The opinion that evolution can produce conditions adverse to environmental adaptation is an instance of this. Adaptation is progress; nonadaptation is devolution and does not promote endurance. Many scientists say natural selection, as likely as not, will approve the nonadaptive; science does not question the omniscient; and error wedges an entry.

303

Any creature that has a brain thinks, however rudimentarily; for the brain is a survival faculty that functions by thinking. The weaverbird was born with a genetic aptitude for learning to weave a nest; the beaver was born with an aptitude for learning to build a lodge. Their having a genetic aptitude does not mean these animals do not have to think to do these things; a crow, failing to fish food from a tube with a wire, bent the end of the wire into a hook and obtained the food. Man differs from these animals only in being born with a more complex mentality, with a genetic aptitude to learn to do more things, to think more extensively.

304

We learn best by teaching, and one remembers for a lifetime that which one has tried to teach others. This fact should be assimilated in some form into teaching methodology. Ingenious teachers should devise some way of getting the students to put real effort into teaching one another. See thought number 445 to learn how the Japanese have done this.

305

A survey of all the conveyers of words reveals to me that the book is the most economical and convenient vehicle to effect at once the preservation, transportation, and dispensation of art contrived of words. A book holds words for centuries as they were printed, can be easily carried in hand or pocket, can be read at no expense, and can be beautifully bound.

306

The philosophies of Kant, Schopenhauer, and their followers assume the human mind runs on a stabilizing track of reason. It doesn't. This track they take to be the a priori parts of cognition (knowledge acquired through innate reasoning ability, prior to experience). The rationalists, to prove the necessity of a priori reasoning, point to the entities of being, unity, substance, cause, and the principle of noncontradiction as necessary for knowledge and inaccessible to experience. All these entities, however, can be experienced by a baby playing with blocks, absorbed as it absorbs nourishment from food, subconsciously in the deep study of play.

307

That thought is congruent with speech is evidenced by the naturalness of a cry of fear or distress when those emotions are provoked. These sounds are instinctively made by the victim and as instinctively understood by others of the same species. A mother rabbit will understand and come to the rescue of one of her kits when she hears its cry of distress. The sounds used in rabbit language to denote a plea for help make use of inflection of tone, beginning in a high tone and curving down to a plaintive ending. With the addition of consonants and vowels, a plea for help in a similar situation, made in English, uses the same inflection of tone; and the sounds used by the Chinese make extensive use of tone in everything they say. Tone is in fact one of the most useful constituents of any language, suggesting that man, like the rabbits, used a tone language before he began to use consonants and vowels.

The sense of hearing and the sound-making apparatus of all animals, including man, evolved as survival faculties and are implications that all animals that have these capacities have an innate aptitude for vocalizing and understanding sound; that is, for language. And language, necessary for the redirection back to the brain of the brain's demands of itself, implies that all animals, to the extent they use language, think.

308

The sound of music and the sense of smell can cast an aura of romance around a person, evidently by instinct. The sense of taste can intrigue and the sense of feel can excite, but in more animalistic ways. Vision can in every way affect the human psyche; and though vision is not the sole agent of thought, because of the importance of imagery in thought, vision is by far the most important. Even in the congenitally blind, vision functions imaginatively.

309

The face must have been eloquent before the tongue could make interpretable sounds, for the wives and children of human brutes make it their pilot star by instinct still, though every thought or feeling can now be expressed in speech. The laziest dullard loafing about the mall will miss no twitch of brow or flick of the eyelid of the nabob of his bunch, not by industry consciously applied, but by industry genetically endowed, an atavistic residuum of countless primordial wars.

310

Sounds evoke mental images of color, size, form, and action. Because of the different sounds in their languages, a race speaking one language sees a different world than a race speaking another.

311

Hegel's dialectic of thesis, antithesis, and synthesis makes a very likely cause of the vanishing of the dinosaurs 300,000,000 years ago. It is most likely that the giant lizards (thesis), during the many millions of years of their predominance on Earth, gradually built up their own impediment (antithesis) to such a degree that a compromise (synthesis) became necessary. There is evidence that a form of mammal evolved that was very fond of dinosaur eggs. Assuming this to be so, perhaps another form of lizard, who loved to eat these mammals, kept the mammalian number within non-threatening proportions. However, the dinosaurs were very fond of eating these mammal-eating lizards; and as the population of dinosaurs became greater, the lizards became fewer, which allowed the egg-loving mammals to prevail to such an extent that the dinosaurs were no longer able to reproduce; and so the mammals became the dominant species.

312

Wisdom is the ability to detect the possible ways to solve a problem.

313

Because every person by reaction to experience makes his own world and no two persons make identical worlds, no person makes his world as the world actually is. Immanuel Kant called the world as it actually is the "world-in-itself." This world-in-itself is simply objective reality; that is, reality not modified by subjective thought. Kant deemed any objectively real thing (any thing-in-itself) beyond the reach of human analysis. However, regardless of its unknowability the world as it really is, is the world to which we must adapt in order to exist. Kant, conceding this, called the items of knowledge in the world-in-itself that are available to the mind of man *a priori*—*deducible,* that is, by human reasoning alone, without recourse to experience. The items of *a priori* knowledge are deducible, according to Kant, by innate faculties in the human mind. The ability to understand them is genetically programmed, not learned.

In spite of all this sophistry, the problem of the inaccessibility of the world-in-itself is easily soluble. The solution is this: the world-in-itself is not inaccessible. Objective reality is accessible for all to see and appears the same to all. No two people, however, give it the same interpretation. The cause of this disparity lies in inevitable difference in any two people's formative experiences. To say that nothing appears the same to any two people is a very loose expression. One could more accurately say nothing has the same value or meaning to any two people, and a thing has value or meaning according to what one sees it in relation to.

I expect Kant would view with disconcertion or, more likely, with contempt the statement that the human mind is a survival faculty and not a philosophical instrument; but so it is. Man's world is a world of fantasy, not necessarily true, but extremely sensitive to necessity. Man may believe a bolt of lightning is the sword of Jove, but this in no way constrains his effort to evade it. A determined adherence to his conception of truth would render man too intransigent to survive the geologic and climatic changes to which a planet swimming in space is subject. Man's mind is not programmed to value objective reality except as it bears on the question of survival. This circumstance necessitates a strict awareness of objective reality, though every person makes his own construction of it.

314

We are necessarily creative when we read, because words do not supply the imagery that must concretize meaning. This imaging, forced on the reader, activates his mind and sets him in the creative mode. Once in the creative mode, the reader goes on to analogy and esthetic enjoyment. This stimulates the entire function of the imagination, giving healthy exercise to the neurons in the brain that generate creative thought.

315

E-mail writing discourages good writing in favor of expeditious writing, and it will prevail among the people because of the appreciation of dispatch insinuated by the quick automation of modem technology as well as because of the natural compliance of all living creatures with the rule of parsimony. This easy adoption of perfunctory verbal expression conduces to perfunctory thinking; for, in spite of the efforts of modem psychology to instate learning on a higher and more esoteric level than mere vice, learning is habit formation; and so essential is language to thought that, without it, man could have no more thought control than the beasts of the jungle. The brain controls the body; nothing controls the brain, save language, by the control of which the brain can control itself. Controlling language as an external force, the brain makes language an external stimulator of the brain's self-control.

316

An achievement never brings one as much happiness as was anticipated, for one must earn it. Deserving an achievement diminishes it by comparison with one's supposed ability. The expression "only what he deserves" betrays the social acknowledgment of this diminution. It is the fantasized achievement before it happens that delights—the dreaming of it.

317

What a person writes or says is not exactly what it is; it's exactly what he means it to be. Critics look at what a writer writes and start giving it names. This is wrenching from context. To know, or at least to get a better idea of exactly what the author means, they would have to ask the author what he means by it; and they could come closer to his exact meaning by discussing it with him. An author tries to leave his meaning exactly in his words, but this is impossible, for no word means the same to any two people. A word does not contain meaning; a word is a construct the reader fills with meaning. A reader puts his own meaning into the words he reads; and just as no two readers can read the exactly same book, so no one can read the exact book the author writes. He may read a better book, for the author has supplied the constructs he need but fill.

318

People can signal with face language without drawing immediate vocal response, for a person can read a face message without letting the sender know he understands it. Face language is a language parallel to a spoken language, a paralanguage. Like the ability to learn to build a nest enjoyed by birds, the ability to learn to read the face is genetically programmed. Nevertheless, because less susceptible to mistaken interpretation, our spoken language takes precedence over our face language. In ordinary society we can successfully deny what the face says.

319

From my lakeside apartment, while the female ducks were off nesting, I noticed the drakes frequently raping an old female duck who was too old and feeble to prevent them. One drake, who had sprained his foot, was unable to catch even this old female. Another male, when finished raping the old female, dismounted, but held her till his crippled companion had hurried up and secured her and so got his satisfaction also. However unsavory by human standards, this behavior shows sympathy and extended thought in animals beyond pure instinct.

320

There is probably more synergism in the world than we have commonly supposed. The thirty or so separate muscles in the human face, something like eighteen separate muscles in the neck, and even the several muscles in the head flex severally much or little or remain motionless all together to create a synergistic unity of expression that other humans and even some of the higher animals, especially dogs, are genetically programmed to interpret, the animals perhaps in a very fundamental way, but humans in a very intricate, complex, and accurate way. Even many inorganic entities function synergistically. The sun, for example, the soil, water, air, the rate at which the earth turns, and no telling what else synergize to feed every organism on earth. Many inanimate entities synergize in more than one operation at once: ripe wheat makes a hiding place for baby rabbits.

321

With their imagination the blind form what they can't see. Even we who can see improve on reality with our imagination, and the blind are not distracted by sight, as we are.

322

Pilate, when he asked, "What is truth?" did well to hurry away; for the question is meaningless. As well ask, "How tall is a tree?" We universally think of truth as a condition or circumstance, like a scientific fact, to be discovered. It's not. Truth is like a work of art, to be created. It makes sense only to ask, "What do you make truth to be?" for everyone has to create his own world. Reality is chaos, and every person must build his own order of it. The behavior of every sane person must be recognizable as human by other humans because we must cooperate with each other in order to survive. We must also recognize other humans as human beings; so by the degree to which we, in general, resemble each other, we can ascertain the degree to which our creations of order are similar. They are just similar enough for us to achieve the cooperation necessary for the survival of our species. They have to be as different as possible because the opposition factor (the tendency of every person to oppose the opinion of every other person) is necessary for our survival also. The opposition factor functions by causing many different solutions to our important problems to be advocated, increasing our chances of finding the right solution. Thus the unavoidable ambiguity of interpersonal communication is as essential to our survival as the efficient clarity with which we talk to ourselves. The confusion is the soil from which grows disagreement and all the diverse solutions we apply to our problems.

323

Long use of the corrugating muscles of the face can give one a permanent expression and provide a clue to one's character and personality.

324

One is different at different times and often finds one's conclusion drawn earlier to be wrong. In light of this, one's dudgeon on being found wrong by others, who are always different than one, is evidence of egotistically skewed judgment.

325

We have a dilemma in free enterprise: money is automatically transduced to political power, but the ability to get money does not entail the ability to wield power wisely. The only way out of this dilemma is to persuade the citizenry to put a limit on the amount of money one may possess, an unlikely prospect.

326

When one understands a concept, one can accurately anticipate that about it that has not yet been said or read, but only from one's individual perspective. One can never see anything from anyone else's perspective. For that, one would have to see with the other person's eyes, think with the other person's brain. Life is a condition; togetherness is always a pretense.

327

Feeling is all man has besides matter. Man's bones and flesh are completely charged with nerves that carry feelings from every part of his body to the sensitive and retentive feeler, the brain. The senses register effects in the brain that galvanize emotion; and the brain itself, enabled by memory, effectuates thought. That thought is feeling is patently evident simply in that thought affects our emotions. Thinking of a fearful situation, though the situation no longer obtains, can cause the emotion of anxiety; thinking of an insult suffered even years ago causes the emotion of anger, and our feelings are hurt when we think of humiliating treatment we have received. All these reactions happen because these thoughts *are* anxiety, anger, and humiliation.

328

Shakespeare's sonnets give no new information; but like the painter's art, adds charm to a familiar scene. The poet, by the use of rhyme, rhythm, and a special euphonic diction that is his by peculiar talent, helps the reader appreciate the things the reader knows familiarly and well, enriching segments of every person's life. It is the province of art to deepen and flavor feeling. There is no place in poetry for obscure meaning, for unfamiliar idiom, or, except in an occasional transient and refreshing counterpoint, for jerky, unrhythmic diction. The word-puzzles of bunched prose that pass for poetry in the magazines of today (2009) are probably the least read of all printed works. A poet does not grow on every bush.

329

Nothing is of so great value to man as his ability to formulate and control thought with words. In reading, our creative faculties are aggrandized by exercise; for we have to create the images that concretize the meanings of words. Writing is even more creative than reading; for in writing we must choose the word that will evoke images in the mind of the reader that are as like as possible to the images we mean to convey. That we will convey the exact images that are in our own mind (which would be ideal) is so improbable as to be impossible; for that would require the writer and reader to have had the same experiences and to be in the same frame of mind. Interpersonal communication is therefore necessarily imperfect.

But interpersonal communication is not the primary function of language. Though primary importance to the survival and predominance of the human species, the importance of the communication we have with others runs a poor second to the communication we have with ourselves. By *intra*personal communication, using internalized language (language of such accustomed use that it is used subconsciously and is indistinguishable from thought), one improvises and structures reality, organizes thought, achieves an identity, and establishes intention. One is always in one's own presence and concerned with one's own activities and problems. One's idleness is constant self-appraisement. Comparatively, one seldom talks to others; and when one does, one's exchange is brief and of little interest. For nature evolves with unfeeling efficiency: every creature can best guide and protect the creature that resides within its own skin, and language is the indirect stimulator by the use of which the mind (which can stimulate only things other than itself) can stimulate itself. It's the tool by moving which the mover (that can move only things other than itself) can move itself.

330

Two entities the obscurantist uses are words and the interrelation of words, or syntax. They are two of the holes through which he can escape clarity without being called to account There are words and word uses that a person for whom the obscurantist is writing or talking could be expected to understand and to follow the use of; but just a few degrees more esotericism puts his words beyond the understanding of a majority of even this presigned audience. From there it is easy to go imperceptibly into words and word uses the obscurantist has invented himself and of which no one else has ever heard or dreamed. The obscurantist can then pretend that others who are as bright as he should be able to pick up the meanings and uses of these invented terms if they are understanding what he is saying and even, as he obviously expects them to do, understanding what he is leaving unsaid. Thus the obscurantist escapes into a fantastic chaos of words and unidiomatic word uses that no one could possibly understand, but that no one will confess not understanding for fear of revealing to all that one is what one has always feared one was: intellectually deficient. This is a deep and unconscious fear that nearly all of us have. It enables the obscurantist to achieve, also unconsciously, his desire to be the only one in the room who knows what he is talking about. This gives him a feeling of superiority, which he needs because he, especially, is endowed with the unconscious fear that he is mentally deficient. There are other devices the obscurantist uses, such as far-fetched analogies or jumping over bits of essential information, implying by appropriate cues that the audience or reader has of course got it; and I have even heard the crude stratagem used of dropping the voice to an inaudible whisper for the last three or four words of a sentence. This simple artifice is obvious to all except the obscurantist himself, for he is achieving his object unconsciously.

331

Pain is an effective teacher. It's not a good teacher, however, for it doesn't encourage the student to learn.

332

We say we have free will because we don't know of any force that causes us to think as we do, and it is precisely because our will is free that we don't know this. It is at the source of decision that decision cannot be observed. We cannot feel the brain because the brain is the source of feeling. It feels for the body; there is nothing to feel for the brain. In like manner, we make the decision for our actions; there is nothing to make the decision for us. An actor, to learn whether his acting is good, must ask a member of the audience.

333

I believe man's will is ultimately free but is strongly influenced partly directly or indirectly from outside the mind, by experience, and partly from inside the mind by genetically-based tendencies. The amount of internal vs external influence depends on the amount of socialization vs individualization to which a person has been subject. What he is free to do depends on his capacity for behavioral control, which depends on his capacity for autostimulation by the use of internalized language.

334

All interpersonal communication instrumental to immediate response requires immediate feedback, and recorded communication lacks immediate feedback. Lacking immediate feedback, recorded telephone messages are never satisfactory. They make the caller listen to much detail, nearly all of which could not possibly be any of the caller's concern. After wasting the caller's time in this way, they tell him to leave a message and they will get back to him as soon as possible. They also drastically limit what the caller's message can be, and some demand prerequisite information from the caller that he will in all probability have to do research to find. Further, some of the recorded delivery is so rapid and/or ill-pronounced that the caller cannot understand, especially those who are slow thinkers or elderly; and of course there is no way to request repetition.

335

Recorded messages are obviously employed to benefit the establishment that has installed them and/or to frustrate the callers who must use them; for those who install them cannot be unaware of the extreme frustration they occasion.

336

An artist was exhibiting his painting of an old man chopping wood on a winter's day. In response to the often posed question, "What are you trying to say in this painting?" the artist said, "I mean to say the imagination of man could be put to valuable uses if he were trained to master it and to sensitize it, and that the use of the imagination should be a required undergraduate course in all colleges and universities. I mean also to list a few of the uses to which it could be put and to refer the viewer to Seneca's words on the subject of the imagination. Do any of you get this from it?"

When the viewers, who had been stricken wordless recovered speech, one said, "I may be stupid, but I confess I can't see any of that in it."

"You mean," cried the artist, "that I have painted this whole picture in vain? Then I might as well destroy it [taking it from the wall]. Shall I destroy it?"

"No, no!" the viewers cried in chorus, "Don't destroy such a work, by any means!"

'Well, then," said the artist, returning the painting to its place on the wall, "when you tell me why I should not destroy it, you will have answered your question as to what I am trying to say by painting it."

337

The reason a social worker cannot get the natives of a primitive society to change as soon as he shows them a better way to live or to work is that he hasn't affected their private worlds. They live within the ways to which they have become habituated like the snail lives within the shell it has grown. Their great desire is not for efficiency, but for the acting out of their old habitual ways. To them this is a ritual of beauty. Turning the light on ourselves, why do we put *ugh* in the word *thought?*

338

We live in an intellectual bubble filled with the concepts that we believe attend existence. Beyond the limits of that bubble is the infinite space of the unknown. Since all of our beliefs about the infinite space of the unknown are believed on no evidence, any of our beliefs about the infinite unknown is as correct as any other.

339

We could profit by studying abstracts of past experiments and applying them to analogous situations. Call it retroexperiment.

340

It is my opinion that all memory is the same, dependent entirely on the strength of the relevant impression and not on any distinction between short and long memory.

341

Good literature, when appreciated, stirs the human sensorium deeply with ideas beautifully expressed. It reveals thus powerfully how people of the highest level of culture have felt about and reacted to human experiences. It transmits these feelings to those who read. Literature is the art that promotes civilization. Other courses of study tell about civilization; literature, by identification and imagined experience, transmits the habit of it.

342

Whether one grows wiser as one grows older should be determined in regard to something all know how to do and virtually all do, in order to eliminate knowledge as a determining factor. Driving a vehicle on the public highways meets this requirement, and the evidence is that the older are wiser. Young drivers more often drive too fast, drive under the influence of a drug or intoxicant, drive recklessly or carelessly, and have more accidents than older drivers.

343

Memory is not confined to any one part of the body, but is in all parts that contain nerves. In dancing, the feet often remember what the head has forgotten; and in typing or playing a stringed instrument, the hands remember. They amaze the performer as though they had a head of their own. These memories are not retained in the brain subconsciously, for the brain cannot recall them at some later time, while they are available at all times to the hands and feet.

344

Man mistakes the nature of his intelligence. He thinks it is a condition dependent on only his genes and brain. His genes are indeed its foundation and his brain its repository; but his intelligence is dependent on his ability to use language, his ability, especially, to talk silently in imagination to himself. By this self-counsel, driven by long use into the subconscious and recognized as thought, he can believe the most evil or stupid behavior is virtuous or wise. He can believe this also by the counsel of others. Words lead his thought as on a path that is posted with directions. Words cause him to imagine a matter as it is described. Arranged syntactically, words provide man with an intellectual structure that, after training in their uses and at some expense to his meaning, hold him to his subject and guide him to his objective.

345

We have a very primitive need to force others to agree with our private thoughts, because thought is feeling. Denial of something we believe is an intellectual injury. This circumstance adds urgency to our need to come to terms with psychic engulfment, the erroneous belief that our world is the world of all. Adolf Hitler is the archetype of submission to this primitive and common need.

346

The reason Alexander von Humboldt discovered a narrower window of temperature tolerance when the body is acclimated to warm weather is that, in warm weather, the blood stays near the surface of the body, for cooling, and sensitizes the skin; so the body is more sensitive in warm weather.

347

Originally, there was a form of life, which, through the compromise of adaptation, was left with survival faculties, of which the brain was one. The brain is an extremely sensitive, extremely retentive feeler. Its action is the mind. The mind consists of the reaction of material to conditions of other material. It is only the complexity of intelligence that causes us to think of the mind as some mysterious, fairy thing apart from mundane matter. It's all matter.

348

One cannot lose oneself completely in the text of what one reads, for one must keep a certain amount of self-control in order to read. No such constraint affects one who is watching television; one is transported into the world depicted on the screen, engrossed, unthinking, a transitory nonentity.

349

The face is so responsive to the feelings that when two people have lived together for many years, have become thoroughly identified with one another, and have shared the same experiences for so long that they have much the same feelings, the muscles of facial expression become set so as to hold their faces in such a way that they resemble each other. This resemblance is partly due also to the action of the facial muscles, to the way the facial expression changes.

350

It has long been an innocent sport at parties for young folk to form a circle and laugh at the changes a whispered message has undergone after traveling around the circle. The image is prior to the word for the speaker; the word comes first for the listener. The communicative words are common to all, but the images that manifest their meanings are the listener's private own in all cases, and no two people interpret the same words with the same imagery. Inevitably, therefore, any message that passes through many minds is garbled. The best minds could do no better than to study to improve interpersonal communication.

351

Science uses numbers, not as a new language, but as words in our old language. Mathematical symbolism is not a nonverbal instrument, as George Steiner called it. In "3 cows,""3" is an adjective, and when we pronounce it we use the word *three*. Of higher mathematics I wouldn't want to speak, for I know nothing about higher mathematics, but all mathematics is only another intellectual area the mind has made. The mind envelopes science just as it does every other subject that man understands. Symbols are a shorthand way of writing words pronounced *dash, period, asterisk, hyphen, dagger, swung dash,* or *curl* or *tilde* or *negation symbol.* All the words of a language are also symbols. The jargon of science is not about to displace language. It *is* language. And language envelopes science, which is only a segment of man's knowable world.

352

When we experience a person only in his public mode of behavior, we can be grossly misled as to his intellectual depth. Since the public world is a wide but shallow world, a person can have social skill and yet have a very shallow mental capacity; and people are often hired to fill positions that require intellectual depth who have only social skill to recommend them. Others are hired to fill positions that require social skill because they have demonstrated intellectual ability. I expect there are not many who are equally capable in both the private and public modes of behavior, for skill in one of these modes augurs against skill in the other. Extroversion augurs against introversion. They are opposite personalities.

353

The impact of life and reality on the newly-formed and very sensitive nervous system of the newly born and even the prenatal human infant stimulates the impulse to understand and react, resulting in the analogical expression of feelings by physical agitation, striving for more intense realization, which results in the partial formulation of meaning, leaving the nervous system extremely inclined to culminate the already begun adaptation to the immediate environment, which violently stimulates the entire infantile organism. The kinetic and haptic sensations in the prenatal and the vocalized sounds of the newly born, some imaginary and some audible, assume the function of formulating by sound the desires for adaptation to and understanding of the infant's immediate surroundings. Endless repetitions of this exercise, together with the habituating effect of all action, results necessarily, because the baby thinks, in the development of a distinct and unique private language, understandable by the user alone.

354

To be able to think in regard to something, one has to know words that relate to it. Thus, the very nucleus of learning is acquiring the meanings of words, creating, that is to say, one's personal version of the images words have been decreed to evoke. For the pursuit of learning in any field of study, therefore, the heart of a university is its library and the prime learning tool is a dictionary.

355

Apropos of evolution, scientists talk as though nature met man's needs, as though the mold changed to take the form of the object being molded. Rather, as any scientist would affirm, man conformed to nature's requirements.

356

Man's desires have a startling effect on his reactions to reality. We would be horrified by a disease that killed as many as traffic accidents, but we blink at traffic accidents as though unaware that the next death may be our own.

357

The commonest attribute of interpersonal communication is misunderstanding. In fact, only the crudest exchange of information between individuals can be made without some misunderstanding. So much the greater part of the self-conscious orientation of every individual must be maintained through conception and action with an egocentric focus that intrapersonal communication soon builds a very complex interrelation of habitual reactions, defenses, and mental attitudes. These are within the mind of one person; no one else is privy to them; and every person has a like unique cognitive complexity. Between two minds, the innumerable differences that gradually become established during long years of isolated self-study and attempted betterment make a perfect agreement on any one mental detail a virtual impossibility.

The only perfect communication is intrapersonal, for the communicator and cornmunicatee are then the same. Self-counsel formulates thought, reconnoiters reality, and anchors sanity. Nature stamps it the most important use of language by its compatibility with the centrality of life force in every form of life.

358

I think it probable that tone was important in man's communication early in his evolution. Perhaps his first language was a tone language. Many animals communicate with tones, and tones seem to be instinctively used by humans in moments of crisis. This, to me, suggests there was a time when tone was the only conveyance of information; and this suggestion is strengthened by the results of such experiments as the one performed by Dr. Michael Posner and Brenda Patoine in May, 2009, in which student IQ scores were improved by training in music. Also, the use of tone by the Chinese is probably residual from time immemorial.

359

Transformation, synergism, adaptation, and inertia are four great earthly regulatory factors. They apply to inorganic as well as to organic matter. Water is transformed to ice by the synergistic effects of sun, the earth's revolution and wobble, and the chemical composition of water. Soil, water, and sunlight synergistically produce flora. Facial expression is made by the synergistic effects of the mouth, the muscles around the eyes, the eyebrows, and the other muscles of facial expression. Adaptation keeps things from breaking against superior force. It allows blades of grass to bend all one way in a high wind, no matter which way the individual blades are wont to lean. It allows dogs and cats, basically wild animals, to live perfectly well as pets in a human family. It allows man to form habits (and therefore to learn). It allows him, although he has inescapably a unique private world, to live wholly, or almost wholly, in the public world when adversity threatens his species. It allows children to learn efficiently from poor teachers and parents. It allows people to get along pretty well together and society to go along pretty smoothly. It prevents philosophers and psychiatrists from making too many hard and fast rules of human behavior. Inertia prevents a too ready occurrence of transformation, synergism, and adaptation. Inertia constitutes a considerable part of prudence.

360

Man is proportioned much like every creature that evolved in the same environment as he. Animals and even insects have heads with eyes, ears, nose, and mouth positioned and functioning like man's; and the conditions that make all earthly creatures physically alike make them also mentally alike. The animal brain evolved as the fittest faculty to protect the animal from the same hazards as man's brain evolved to protect man. Oral capability and otic sense make two of the prime survival faculties; inter- and intra-communication is common to all.

361

In the sense of considering something apart from a concrete instance, man cannot think. Therefore, man cannot think in the abstract. He uses symbols, in the form of words, which anchor and formulate all thought, as concrete stepping stones to make his way over all degrees of abstraction. Symbols elicit mental images, which concretize concepts. To think in the abstract would be to think without mental images, which would be to think without thought; for we think with mental images.

362

To have a thought one must first find the words to express it to oneself.

363

The little daily chores that bore us make a moderation that increases our happiness. They force us to a moderation we should choose ourselves. With the excess of time we would have without them we would be unhappy. The measure of enjoyment is of course the measurement only of how things seem. You make yourself happy by making yourself unhappy; you have relativity; use it! Appetite is the best sauce. White looks twice as white against a black ground. You can double your pleasure by throwing half away.

364

If a tree falls in the forest with no normal ear to hear it, it makes no sound; although there is the reverberation of the air that would make sound in someone's ear. It requires the very complex hearing apparatus of an ear to make sound of reverberating air.

365

Should people stage funerals and see their loved ones dead? This is a question for psychological consideration.

366

At this time (2009), I am eighty-six. I used in my youth and middle age to see death as a going down into smothering darkness. Now, looking back over a long life of struggle to make a living, to fight off the occasional encroachment of disease, and manage all the arrangements necessary in daily life, I can't help viewing death as an acceptable inevitability.

367

To seek a place with many attractions at which to read or to conceive and write ideas is like trying to better understand a lecture by accompanying it with loud music. In reading or writing we function in the world of the mind; the enticing actual environment serves only as distraction. One can appreciate the mental world most when the material world is least attractive. The famous author Flannery O'Connor had her desk in a corner of a room, facing the corner.

368

The primary purpose of the jury is not to achieve justice, but to prevent executive tyranny; that is, to assure the litigant that he is being judged by his peers and is not being done dirty by sophisticated law persons. A jury can legally be a very ignorant group of people. And the purpose of punishment is not primarily to condition the defendant, but to preserve the ethnic balance; that is, to preserve the balance between the inclinations of individuals and the security expected from social institutions (see Susanne K. Langer, *Mind,* Volume III, page 125). This about punishment, I believe, is understood by very few.

I believe the judiciary branch of government should be acting to find a way to achieve justice without offending the litigants and to make better citizens of the convicted defendants without disturbing society.

369

The live human being is essentially mental. A person should therefore get to know a friend or lover by written correspondence before he or she has ever seen the other. This will let him or her know what sort of person he or she is getting. Seeing the other would inevitably bias the impression. The physical impression, when the two have become accustomed to each other, will vanish like the sense of smell after the olfactory sense is exhausted; while the mental compatibility will only become more patently evident.

370

Words can have an onomatopoeic origin by analogy to different sensory stimulants. In England, one wearing a long, sad woebegone expression is said to be wearing a po face. *Speed* sounds like a flying object; *rock* like a hard object. Many word origins must be thus analogously derived, not surprisingly, since all words are essentially metaphors and all our thinking is finally formulated by language. The word *bull* is another word probably both onomatopoeically and analogously conceived. The sound of it overlaps with the conception of an arrogant push of overwhelming force, as in "bull market," and "a bull move." The opposing concept of fearfulness has spawned the British word *frit* (nf) as well as, probably, the common word *timorous*. Also, the L and F sounds of the word *leaf* have qualities in common with leaves. If we admit onomatopoeic metaphor, language may, after all, be mainly onomatopoeically created.

371

I recently read a precept written by a famous philosopher to the effect that people are in general insufficiently aware that a theory is easily formulated; but when it comes to its practical application, a number of unforeseen difficulties invariably arise. The timeliness of this message brought to my mind our dangerous highways and our recorded telephone messages that are so neatly planned and so often frustrating to use. The name of my famous informant was Epictetus (c. 55-c. 135 AD), and my purpose in writing this thought is to impress anyone who reads it with the gross error inherent in rejecting writers on grounds of archaism. Except on subjects such as discovery, or fashion, the writers of past time repay perusal. Modern writers cannot be expected to have all the knowledge past writers had, plus all that has been learned since. To avoid the writers of the past is to discard much of man's progress.

372

Because no two people could have the same formative experiences, no two people could possibly have identical conceptions of the same world. Therefore, to be in love with a person is to have built a wholly imaginary fantasy of which that person is the material core. Better acquaintance will alter the fantasy for at least one, and probably for both the lovers. The wise *engage* will consider this before marriage.

373

The energy that exercises the instinct of a spherical stone to role is always from outside the stone; so its rolling instinct is not what we call a need. However, most instincts of an animal are energized from inside the body, and we call them needs. Just being round does not make a stone want to roll; but just having a hard head and bulging muscles and a brain designed for their exercise does make a bull want to butt.

374

The shortest arc portends the most perfect circle.

375

The many superstitions of a primitive people excuse them for the many tragedies in their lives. Magic spirits are to blame when someone dies or becomes ill. These shock absorbers satisfy the instinct to emotionally survive catastrophe. Even today religion serves this purpose for many. For many, faith makes any atrocity warrantable if the Lord did it.

376

The brain evolved faster than the cranium due to need for earlier survival capability in a perilous environment; and today, because it adds neurons in reaction to new information, it is hurried along by the computer and television, growing far faster than the cranium and becoming too tight. We should study the killer whale, whose longer earthly existence makes its brain tighter than man's (See *Principles of Brain Evolution,* by Gorg F. Striedter, page 357).

377

Memory is achieved by association. Several different types of stimulation peculiar to the entity to be remembered affect the sense receptors of a cognitive creature, which establishes a variegated associative relationship between the entity and the cognitive creature. The more different types of stimulation and the more impressive the stimulations, the greater the duration of the memory.

378

If one is moderately depressed or disturbed and cannot get one's thoughts away from the depressing or disturbing subject, one should read in a book; for where one's attention is, is where one is mentally. Preferably, one should choose a book of humor whose humor is based on what is commonly called "a way with words," the prototype of which is the books of P. G. Wodehouse. One of such books can profitably be kept handy, in the manner of a medicine, to treat cases of mild anxiety or depression. For anything short of clinical depression, this is a very effectual corrective.

379

A person's environment is part of one's concept of that person. If one has seen that person in only one place, one may not recognize the person in an unaccustomed place until one has seen and recognized the person in more than one place. Thus subconscious mental flanges frame cognition.

380

It is my opinion that all learning is the same, the inculcation of matter by review, no matter how the review is accomplished.

381

I expect during the evolution of man human children, especially girl children, were so often savagely destroyed by a male parent in a fit of pique that the special endearing qualities and characteristics that would lessen the likelihood of this became hardwired very early by natural selection in the cerebral circuitry of the survivors (any who survive are considered selected by nature). It is confidently supposed that, because of constant wars between tribes, boy children were preferred; and one can imagine that only very alluring girl children were likely to survive father's emotional ups and downs. Commensurate with this supposition is the fact that girl babies, more than boy babies, react to attention by adults with eager and pretty smiles.

382

What we know of past and present we call reality; what we project of the future we call fantasy. Both our knowing and our projecting are necessary. Reality and fantasy are joined at the prow of the present, and both are fantasy, for every person makes his unique picture of reality as well as of the probable future.

383

Because thought is feeling, the ultimate expression of thought is physical action; and, by virtue of this, the more freedom given a society, the more will that society gradually revert to precivilized behavior. I instance ours.

384

Heat makes water boil, and the boiling protects the water from the heat. Cold makes water freeze, and the freezing protects the water from the cold. The eagle makes the jackrabbit develop long legs, and the long legs protect the jackrabbit from the eagle. The jackrabbit, being sensate, finds joy in the exercise of its long and powerful legs. For the exercise of its legs, gamboling with its fellow jackrabbits will suffice; but that is to overlook the fact that the jackrabbit's brain evolved in the same environmental circumstances that built the legs; and the brain can distinguish between a romp with playmates and escape from the eagle. For the brain, the romp will not do; an eagle is required.

385

It is not true that there are exceptions in nature because exceptions cause change and change is essential for survival. Rather, change is essential for survival because there are exceptions in nature and exceptions cause change.

386

One can analyze somewhat of the brain by studying the body, for the evolutionary forces that formed the body also formed the brain.

387

I suggest an ethical government be established and every effort be made to instill in the people the conviction that honoring these ethical laws be the duty of every citizen of this government. The attention of the people will then be not on the obeying of these laws, but on the doing of this duty, by which obeying the laws will be accomplished. The people will never find fault with the ethical laws because their attention will be on the duty. The nature of duty inspires loyalty; pride and integrity are challenged; for the doing of his duty shows what a man is made of, and if one fails an honorable duty, one must live with the memory of it. Inclination will be forgotten, swallowed up in the determination to see duty done honorably and well. Japan has done it (see *Confucius Lives Next Door,* by T. R. Reid). We should be ashamed of both our government and our crime rate. We should honor the Japanese by emulating their astonishing accomplishment.

388

Conflict of adverse instincts can be demonstrated due to the presence of sensitivity throughout the nervous system. I experienced a manifestation of this when I dropped a lid I was putting on a jar of juice. I was holding the jar of juice in my left hand and dropped the lid I was applying with my right hand. My left hand made a short, quick movement, motivated by the instinct to catch the lid, causing me to spill some of the juice. The conflict was between the instinct to save the juice and the instinct to catch the lid. The impulsive consequence of this conflict was unavoidable due to its immediate effect through the neuronal reflex arc. Very common are such instinctive conflicts, though not necessarily involving the reflex arc. A man, for example, may be wanted by his men friends to make a foursome at cards (instinct to be sociable), while his girlfriend wants him to watch TV with her (sexual instinct); or a man might be offered a low-status, high-salary job (instinct for gain) and at the same time a low-salary, high-status job (instinct for social status).

389

Because thought is feeling, thinking was once believed to be a function of the heart.

390

We might find when man started some development that shows in the brain and thus find out approximately how long it takes a development to change the brain to a certain degree. The brain might thus become a sort of archeological clock.

391

Evolution is the elimination by environmental conditions of a chaos of countless alternatives, leaving a sparse few.

392

A spokesman for the Tasaday, a cave-dwelling people on a Philippine island, said their love for their leader was not small, like so (holding up his little finger), but big, like so (holding up his thumb). Thus it appears analogical thinking is basic in the thinking of the most primitive of peoples.

393

A person's religion embeds his most revered values. A study of man's attitude toward various aspects of his religion would be a valuable supplement in the study of his character.

394

Man has an instinct to learn, for his brain is so formed that he can learn.

395

I think the brain has less of what men of science call approximation, generalization, categorization, and degeneration in middle and old age than it has during infancy. If a baby sees any factor common to two different entities or situations, it puts both these entities or situations into the same category. With age one becomes more specific.

396

Because no word could mean quite the same to any two persons, every person, to some degree, uses a private language understood by himself alone. Proof, then, has always been patent that there can be private languages.

397

Man's brain evolved as a survival faculty, not a philosophical instrument. Evolution, however, is still in progress; organisms are constantly adapting to a changing environment. Thinking ability, for example, gives an advantage in the mating game, thereby becoming a genetic constituent of the human psyche.

398

Thought is feeling, a fact that has the rooted corollary that all reasonable thinking has the ultimate object of finding an excuse to behave emotionally.

399

I have found it written by men of science that man's tendency to quarrel for most any reason is a survival faculty developed when man was living by hunting and gathering in order to make sure that groups of hunters would break apart before they became too numerous to survive. This manner of expression leads readers to the common erroneous supposition that evolution progressed according to a previously conceived plan. Factiousness did not evolve in order to make sure of anything. There was no conscious purpose behind its development. It evolved because hunting bands who did not contain enough factious members to keep them from getting too large did not survive to have offspring like themselves. The factious bands were what was left after the too-numerous bands broke up or perished. It would more truthfully have been put that factiousness is a survival process that evolved because hunting bands that remained together soon grew too large to feed themselves.

400

Television drives the minds of the populace toward one level, and one broadcasting station thus enslaves many minds. The level it drives them to is a low one, for the matter broadcast must be understood by all. The principal force it uses is rapidly changing pictures, which disables our ability to think because we think with images. Other seducements, which cannot be practiced with printed matter, are sound and the illusion of movement.

401

With the first ten or fifteen seconds of applause at a classical concert, the audience is saying something about the musicians. With any further applause, they are saying something about themselves; and here they really have something to say. The applause lasts sometimes minutes. If they were really that crazy about classical music, concerts would be so profitable there would be more of them. Communication by act, as by words, is used more often to conceal than to reveal.

402

Marijuana ruins one's life. Because one can sense only relatively, the transport of rapturous delight that marijuana effects renders one's normal feeling of well-being unbearably dull. Many are killed trying to steal marijuana

403

Any body member, as we have long known, grows with use; and we now know this applies even to the brain. The parts grow with use, say we, because of the need to better facilitate their function and put thereby a little more security around the survival of our species. Without thinking very much about it, we assume nature causes the growth of much-used parts to happen through some sort of magic, a kind of thing that only nature understands.

Actually, it's very simple. It happens because the exercise exacerbates the action of the blood in the acting member. It exacerbates the blood action, not because the used part needs such blood action, but because the action of the muscles squeezes blood out of the used part, which, like an expanding sponge, then sucks blood in. The forceful action of the blood more effectively feeds a greater number of cells in the working part. The action has no more magic or intention than a sponge that helps one bathe or clean a window.

404

When a person talks to himself, his interlocutor is a phantom self, an object of his imagination. Everyone has a phantom self. If one's phantom self is worthy enough to be good company, one will never be lonely. One should make his phantom self someone he respects, a worthy counselor. A person can make his phantom self worthy only by making himself worthy. One's phantom self is a reflection of oneself, as in a mirror, but the phantom self is real; for the brain that maintains him is real; and his use is beneficial.

405

An attitude in the family which is conducive to peace of mind, in which both parents wish all to be happy, is very important in raising children without problems which interfere with their social adjustment.

406

Conrad Lorenz says one cannot wish for the destruction of another country if one knows there are people in that country who share even one of one's values (On Aggression, page 292). Did he suppose opposing forces in the American civil war shared no values? The sharing of values is precisely the cause of all wars.

407

To feel joy, one must have experienced the ame-
lioration of a situation that made one unhappy. All our
joy we owe to unhappiness.

408

Chimpanzees make and use tools (grass stems)
to fish termites out of their nests. Because these stems
get broken, the chimps make several and lay them by
as spares. These activities require extended thought
that is, the imagining of situations that are the results
of prior images and the cause of following images.

409

One automatically places a value on everything
one knows or believes, and every item of knowledge
or belief one acquires finds its place in one's constellation of values according as its value compares to
the value one puts on everything else one knows or
believes. Therefore, everything one learns causes an
altering shift and a resettling, of some extent, to occur
throughout one's constellation of values; and, as everyone behaves according to one's values, one's behavior
is changed by everything one learns.

410

Everything we learn changes everything we know, but it should be added that what we know often has an effect on what we learn. We always have a desire to find something consonant with what we already believe, so much so that we remember reading relevant material as we wish it were rather than as it actually was.

411

A cold back causes scary dreams because thought is feeling.

412

The fact that we think with imagery explains the strange imagery we experience in dreams without need for reference to physical needs or emotional desires. In dreams the thought image must often displace the thought it represents and lead the dreaming mind a new direction, upon a new but analogous theme. At the point of this preemption, the dreamer's store of memories, guided by the dreamer's constellation of values, if freely made known, might indeed reveal information germane to the dreamer's inmost identity and deep-seated problems, if there are such. I believe the writings of Sigmund Freud would repay further study than they have yet received.

413

One of the greatest faults in teaching has always been the belief that the student must be given instruction based on what the teacher knows. A common example of this can be found in textual glosses in which understandable terms are given obscure definitions. The teacher's task should be primarily to learn what the student knows and secondarily to learn how the subject material can be integrated into or grafted onto what the student knows. This integration or grafting is automatically accomplished by the Japanese method of students teaching students. I remember reading somewhere long ago of a beginning student, a little boy, in a quandary because unable to grasp the difference between printing and writing. His bewilderment was completely resolved when another little boy, a fellow student, demonstrated for him by writing a word and said, "That's writin.'"

414

The constellation of concepts or cognitive schema or cognitive structure that a person carries around in his head is available to one, to any great extent, only in words. It is with words that one gives meaning to one's experience. The peculiar meanings resulting from one's experiences, and the meanings resulting from the combinations of and interrelationships among meanings, give each individual his unique picture of reality, the contents of it as well as his perspectives of the contents and the different values he places on the different concepts. Thus what man sees in reality, and what he deduces from what he sees, are determined by the words he has learned how to use and how he has learned to use them. Our civilization is based on the dictionary and the grammar book, and reading is our most important branch of learning.

415

Memory is achieved by association. Some sort of stimulation is associated with the entity to be remembered, and that stimulation spreads by association to other sensations, adding other associations to the strength of the same memory. The more and stronger associations the entity establishes, the more deeply entrenched the memory. There is a cross-over of an impression made by some sensation unique to a condition productive of a concept. And a sensation need not in any way resemble the entity it brings to mind. One can be reminded of a most unlikely thought. By exercising one's attention like a spotlight, looking for associations, one finds many associations strangely different than the entity that brings them to mind. I expect, by its generation of a neuron, an experience conditions that neuron to respond to a reexperience of that experience, or to an entity related to that experience by association.

416

The French impressionists often gave their paintings names that said nothing that wasn't prominently implicit in the picture, a practice, I believe, that allows the fullest appreciation of the work; for it in no way diverts the attention of the observer. He can appreciate the verbally inexpressible visual statement the painting makes according to his own inclination, a freedom of the greatest importance among Zen and Tao artists.

417

I think when one finds he likes another person, it is, in part, because of that person's ability to use the "one down" position. A person who is not able to do this is likely to have no friends unless he can find a friend who, for the sake of cordial relations, is willing always to find himself one down. The prototype of the one-up addict might well be Adolph Hitler, as described in *The Young Hitler*, by his self-effacing schoolmate and friend August Kubizek. With Hitler, Kubizek was never allowed to say much; and his opinion was never allowed to stand. The world is full of young Hitlers. His rise to power he owed to the sad condition of Germany after World War One. We have since learned to enrich our fallen foes.

418

All our memories are preserved in packages; every concept is the center of a constellation of associated concepts. The fact that these packages happen in dreams is to be expected. They seem strange in dreams, because they are applied there when our critical faculties are latent, and the packages are usually mixed according to the vaguest and most far-fetched analogies. They are assessed when we are awake and our critical faculties are alert. In dreams, we are experiencing the dream material as experience being lived, not as something remembered, but as something experienced for the first time; and it is as something experienced for the first time that we remember it later, when we are awake, with all our critical faculties alert and functional. Actually, it was a blend of remembered packages long since experienced, but related somehow to present experience - - a mnemic noumenon.

419

We experience a thing somewhat according to our appetite for it in the same way that a shock of electricity is the sharper because of resistance to it. The man in jail experiences freedom in a keener sense, by his remembrance of it and his anticipation of it, than the man who walks the streets unconscious of it. Why is it that I remember as my most enjoyable time of learning that time when I was prevented by the necessity of manual labor from going to the university and could only look into a paperback book of learned writing for a brief time during the weekend? It is because that is when, *within me,* I experienced most fondly the searching after knowledge that I so keenly anticipated some day to do.

420

Like the versatility of the genetic possibilities that allow us to survive in case of environmental change, the cerebral neurons are of almost infinite impressionability. They can experience and remember an infinitude of qualia only a small percentage of which we have words to designate or of which we can remember the cause. This is why we can dream of experiences we don't remember having had. Our subconscious swarms with myriads of qualia acquired in experiences merely dreamed, and many of them dreamed in the private language unconsciously created by us in our prenatal stage of development while trying desperately to develop the instinctive faculty of thought.

421

An important factor in reading is that the reader does not feel he is taking the one down position that he might be taking if he were listening to someone talking. The information comes to the reader more as a suggestion; and he rather looks on it as being of his own invention. He does not feel he is being led unwillingly along someone else's familiar path.

422

Our memories confuse similar things because engrams (memory traces) can be wakened by experiences that are similar to the experiences that first established them. This causes us to confuse similar memories, but it is also conducive to creativity, for it is automatic analogy.

423

Opposition is always necessary. We could not reach out our hands without opposing muscles, and we could not think without assessing opposing thoughts. Since opposing opinions within one mind is a source of neurosis, we are normally all a little neurotic.

424

The reason workers are happier on Thursday than they are on Monday is that we experience things relatively. The more intervening time there is between a prior condition and a present condition, the weaker the effect of the prior condition on the present condition. The time intervening between Friday and Monday is greater than it is between Wednesday and Thursday.

It is for the same reason that prisoners, after years of prison life, develop a dread of regaining their freedom. The intervening time between freedom and the prisoner's realization of his present state is long; so that he sees his present state of imprisonment not in relation to freedom, but in relation to imprisonment.

425

Philosophy, since time immemorial, together with modern scientific research maintains that we think with imagery (see Kosslyn, *Image and Brain,* 1994), and given that we do, the images concocted by the brain in dreams, free of the dictates of reality, should tell us something about the way we think. Everything the brain can do awake, it does in dreams; and the dream images are closely related to what the brain is doing, a symbolic representation of it. One can study one's own brain through study of one's dream images.

426

If one desires happiness on earth, he would do well to make use of the fact that one thinks relatively. Of this fact there is the important corollary that something can be changed by changing something else that relates to it. This principle can be demonstrated in a painting: sunlight can be made to seem brighter by putting dark shadows near it.

427

While reading today, I read the word *follows* where it was not written. It happened as follows. I read to the end of a line, then, shifting my vision to the beginning of the next line, I mistakenly read the word *follows*. I then found the word *follows* was the last word at the end of the line below the one I was reading—at the end of the line I was reading now. I was not aware that I had seen *follows* before I mistakenly read it. I take this as strong evidence of the factuality of subliminal perception.

428

All animals have speech because speech is communication by sound; because natural selection allows no faculties to evolve that are not conducive to survival; because all animals have aural and vocal faculties that we know are used by the animals to communicate with their fellow animals; and because animals couldn't have survived for millions of years if they couldn't have warned their fellow animals when danger threatened. Animal language is simple, but when mortal danger threatens always and from every quarter, simplicity is a necessity.

429

One always automatically and immediately puts a personality with every face or photo of a face that one sees; and when one reads a book that has the author's photo in it, one reads with one's concept of the author in mind. It's more satisfying to read with the author in the back of one's mind that has been created by one's own imagination, projecting from the text.

430

Memory traces of past experiences enrich the vicarious experiences we derive from reading as well as our actual experiences. They also enrich our experiences in dreams. They enrich the experiences we derive from television very little, because to appreciate the effects of a past experience on a present experience requires the free use of the mind, free of distraction and free as to time. Both of these freedoms a moving and sounding medium disallows.

431

Intuition is the power that makes the connections essential in reasoning.

432

To solve a social problem, we should first determine which involved force is greatest; for that will be the determining factor. For example, in the problem of illegal drug sales, the main force is easy acquirement of wealth. Even those capable of only the lowest paying work can quickly become rich by selling illicit drugs. They will never stop trying to do this. The astute move, as we learned dealing with alcohol, is to eliminate the source of illegal wealth by the conditional legalization of drugs. This will not be easy, for profuse bribe money is at risk here. Remember the main force. Officers of the law, also, work for money.

433

I think our putting information into computers that are programmed to point out associations will allow us to make more discoveries. This is because the computer will get away from mental set and the consequent need to finish patterns, which blinds us to much that does not fit the pattern we are trying to finish.

434

Disorder is sometimes an aid to creativity, for it breaks the bonds with the artistic appreciation of sequence and the need to finish patterns. Also with education. Education helps much, but it constrains by forming habits.

435

The brain cannot take orders directly from itself because the brain evolved in response to the need to react defensively to situations outside the psyche. The brain's need to control itself was met after the evolution of a method of reacting to external situations had already been developed; no method of reacting directly to itself was developed during its evolution. It had, then, somehow to receive its own counsel from a source outside the psyche. This need was met by the evolution of language. Language is a form of action the brain directs outward from the psyche but receives aurally as counsel from an external source.

436

When one learns something about someone with whom one is relating, one's environment is changed, and there will be some change in one's behavior. What one learns about the person makes that person to some degree different to one; and to that degree, one who associates with people has a continually changing environment.

437

The expression in the animal face (including the human animal) is not made entirely by the action of the facial muscles. It is made by action of some facial muscles and the inaction of other facial muscles in synergistic relation to them. The same inactive facial muscle can perform an essential part in the expression of different emotions due to changes made in one or more synergistically related active muscle.

438

Preliterate, primitive man, still extant in some parts of the world, needed (and some still need) to evolve a changed attitude regarding reality as opposed to fantasy. With a brain according to our most scientific determinants equal to our own, primitive man was and is held thrall to a belief in magic and wizardry that precludes acceptance of the plainest proof of natural cause and effect (see *Primitive Mentality*, by Lucien Levy-Bruhl, copyright 1923). To primitive man, there is no such thing as accident; everything that happens is caused by magical powers, occult and invisible. If he could but distinguish between the real and the fanciful, the modern world would be open to his exploitation, and he would no longer feel obliged to avenge the death of any who die of whatever cause.

We of the modern world have a similar mote in our eye, of which most are not yet conscious. Some day in the far distant future it may be said of us that, if we could have been made to distinguish between infallible function and fallible function, we would have been saved a great deal of frustration and expense as well as have saved hundreds of lives that were daily lost on our nation's highways. Infallible function, demonstrated by

the computer, is function according to studied and prepared rules and procedures, unerringly accurate, producing or making use of enough and not an iota more
than enough of anything it produces or uses. Fallible
function, well demonstrated by the brain, is function
that includes intention, mistakes, probability, and categorization. And also creativity, for fallible function trades
exactitude for creativity. It created infallible function.
Infallible function cannot be creative because it must
follow the single rule it is given for every action; it has
no other. Fallible function is seldom necessarily exact
because it has no rules to follow. It, like natural selection, is well demonstrated by rainfall. Rain will probably
fall sufficiently on the land because there is so much
rain. It doesn't always fall sufficiently, and sometimes it
falls excessively, but we almost always get enough. Also,
anything new we get we will get by fallible function;
for fallible function, with all its mistakes and irregular
action, eventually tries everything because it has intention. When the human brain thinks, it flashes the spotlight of attention in all directions; and analogy, the key
to creativity, doesn't need much of a likeness to make a
metaphor. Further, every word in any language is a metaphor. We think metaphorically; which is to say, we think
by analogy, creatively.

Infallible function, as we see, is more certain,
efficient, and economical than fallible function.
However, infallible function requires a third parameter.
Besides the instruction and the instructed, it needs

an intelligent being to create the instructions. Fallible function, on the other hand, needs no third parameter and needs intelligence enough only to recognize error and pursue possibilities. Saving intention, this modicum of intelligence is about all that distinguishes fallible function from natural selection, which requires no intelligence at all. Fallible function is one step up from natural selection, however, at least; for it saves a few eons of time.

The most glaring evidence we have that we should appreciate the difference between infallible and fallible function is a consequence of the fact that our highways, designed and constructed by fallible function, direct the drivers that use them by infallible function. The drivers that use them, however, drive by fallible function; and the disorganization of that mode of behavior is a genetically programmed provocation to curiosity, change, and mistakes that makes the drivers restless and takes their attention sporadically off the infallible rules of the road, often with fatal consequences.

A proper reaction to awareness of the two modes of function would obviously be to replace the line of paint that is supposed to separate opposing traffic with a barrier that would mechanically prevent a vehicle's crossing into opposing traffic; for, given enough time, all that can happen will happen.

439

Is it possible for the evolution of the eye to happen? Yes, and the proof of this is that is *has* happened, as anyone can see. Why did it happen? It happened because, given enough time, everything that can happen will happen; and when what happens fits a hiatus, it remains to become a necessary part of the developing entity.

440

Infallible instruction, cold and inanimate spawn of the fallible human psyche, can never be part of the pulsing and reactive human psyche.

441

Two of a species who are mature may become associated through the sex act and spawn a new member of the species who, by combining the complex arrangement of genes on the chromosomes of both parents, may prove far superior to either parent Similarly, a person, by communicating an unexceptional idea in an idle conversation, may add a thought to the constellation of concepts of his communicatee that completes an idea of great practical value. Thus is man's creative progress a constantly fomenting factor.

442

Because every person is exposed to unique formative experiences, every person evolves a unique manner of understanding and using and otherwise dealing with new information. In psychological terms, every person develops a unique "cognitive schema." I will add that every person develops this same manner of behaving in relation to every mental experience to which he is subject, even the most trivial; and that, though he develops categories into each of which he automatically puts a fairly wide range of experiences, he still uses a high degree of discrimination. Very few categories of others overlap his own, and none cover it perfectly. It is inevitable therefore that misunderstanding should be the most common characteristic of interpersonal communication.

443

One common and usually benign example of interface between infallibility and fallibility is in public broadcasting. Though the radio or television commentator acts in the fallible mode, as does the audience in the interpretation of his commentary, the intervening transmission and conversion that makes their communication one-way; that is, the radio, functions infallibly. The commentator may mispronounce and have to repeat a word and any or all of the audience may not hear a word quite correctly and wish they could ask for a repetition, but the intervening transmitter makes no mistakes; and if some of the matter it transmits is wrong, the mistake cannot be corrected before its transmission.

There are conceivable situations in which a mistake in public broadcast communication consequent to interface of infallible and fallible function that would be important; but the usual mistake amounts to a minor irritation, such as an unimportant misunderstanding or radio static. Infallible management of highway traffic, however, as I have commented above, frequently entails the most extreme tragedy. In fact, the misfortunes attributable to our ignorance of the difference between fallible and infallible modes of function are legion. Wherever technology of any kind and human endeavor function together, they illustrate the disjunction between theory and practice.

The fault is not in their use; both are necessary. We must use modern technology because of the tremendous amount of work to be done, and we can't change our fallible manner of functioning because the creativity and adaptability it allows us is essential to our survival in our variable environment. Besides, fallibility is a universal and ineradicable genetic feature of the animal psyche. The fault is our lack of awareness that the infallible and the fallible modes are two incommensurable and ineradicable modes of functioning that we must learn to use together. This we can learn if we can gain this awareness and adjust to the strengths and weaknesses of each mode.

444

The postulation of Immanuel Kant (1724-1804) that duty in consequence of respect for law must replace inclination if a truly ethical society is ever to be developed can be found in practice in Japan (see T.R. Reid, *Confucius Lives Next Door,* copyright 1999). If T.R. Reid, Tokyo Bureau Chief for *The Washington Post,* is to be believed (and I believe him), this sense of duty has made the Japanese general citizenry one of the most law abiding peoples in the world today. Of course the conditions under which the Japanese live are widely different than the conditions under which we live in the USA. An analysis of this difference might do much to explain how their attitudes and behavior would be likely to develop and how we might be induced to adopt a like behavior.

445

Another tribute is due the Japanese for having been able to get students to teach other students, taking advantage of the fact I mention above that one learns best what one teaches others. In thought 304, I suggest that teachers should try to find a way to get students to teach other students; and the Japanese have found a way. The teacher simply divides the class into study groups, each of which group is assigned a certain amount of learning to do in each study session. The students teach each other. It's noisy, but effective.

In my opinion, it is this technique that has done most to keep the Japanese students among the top students of the world in academic excellence. Find the manner in which this study-group system is effected in T.R. Reid, *Confucius Lives Next Door,* chapter five.

Another of our problems is solved by this study-group method: it works best when there are lots of students. This, I suggest, is because the more students, the less the teacher can be used as a resource.

446

An ingenious person is sometimes singly creative, needing no help to broach an analogous line of thought or to sound its depths; but an assembly of persons is always creative, unconsciously and inevitably, though, because perfect understanding between two persons is impossible, seldom in depth. This group-engendered creativity obtains because, since no two persons can have had the same formative experiences, no word can mean quite the same to any two persons. Therefore, though two persons can discuss related subjects, no subject is quite the same to any two persons. Any subject under discussion between two persons is therefore divided into two separate though closely related subjects. As the discussion proceeds and penetrates deeper and more particularly into the subject, each discussant finds his conception of the subject more and more alien to that of his interlocutor. However, each of them has been exposed to a different conception relative to the subject under discussion. Each, in his immediately future solitary moments and away from any adversary such as would make anything in the way of a concession unpleasant, will reconsider the subject in the light of the new ideas he has acquired. He will perhaps correct some ideas of his interlocutor and perhaps some of his own. He will acquire a new conception of the subject, a definitely creative step.

447

The fact that Kwakiutl Indians have no word for war does not mean they are not warlike. Perhaps it means the reverse. The Eskimos have no word for snow.

448

When one laughs at one's own joke, one proves one can talk to oneself.

449

In spite of their myriad differences, all creatures that live on Earth are subject to the same conditions and therefore have to think generally alike. For this reason, their communication with both self and others has to deal with the same sort of life and has to serve the same functions. Dealing thus in the same way with the same ideas makes every language on Earth a version of one language, the earth language. It would increase global understanding to make earth language one; and given time, with global communication by computer and television, this should be possible. The hard part would be deciding which language to adopt.

450

Perilous conditions prevailing during the early evolution of every creature born with brains have brought that creature forth with the fatal flaw that will spell its end. Man, at that time, with every other encephalic creature, was mere food for more advanced carnivorous beasts until versatile genetic recombination happened to produce a mutant with an abnormally rapid cerebral development, independent of the rest of the body. Enabled thus by intelligence to avoid destruction, man now counts time till his brain becomes too tight, the human species gradually becomes extinct, and new beings with brains inherit man's fatal flaw.

451

The nation in least danger of nuclear attack is the nation whose destruction would most impoverish the economy of the attacking nation. Many developing nations enjoy a degree of this safety.

452

The maxim "Might does not make right" is an expression of inclination consequent to human sympathy. What does it matter that might does not make right if it makes necessity? Might does not make right. Right is made by man's imagination. What might makes is whatever is. Malefaction is wrong because civilization influenced society to arrange a correctional system that has more might than the malefactors.

453

If we (or at least those of us who are civilized to an average degree) don't get angry with a person for the reason that he is mentally incompetent and cannot think reasonably, we shouldn't get angry with someone who can think reasonably, but who does an offensive thing during a thoughtless moment. Everyone does a thoughtless thing occasionally. Of the two modes of functioning extant, fallible and infallible, only the infallible (an artificial mode, since it is man-made and is incapable of choice) never makes a mistake. An employer should know before engaging a person that any person can function only in the fallible mode; and when a competent person makes a mistake (which he inevitably will), his employer should be careful to judge him only by his intentions.

454

We see the human mind as an infallibly functioning computer that wants only a little concentration in
order to be filled with discrete operations as infallibly
functioning as the painted lines that are supposed to
separate opposing traffic on our highways. Instead, the
human mind is fallible and creative; and the fallibility
is the substrate that, by allowing the commission of
mistakes, nourishes the creativity. It is when one finds
oneself wrong that one most effectually learns a new
fact. To find oneself right only confirms what one knew
already.

455

Kant's and Schopenhauer's description of the
"thing in itself' (anything that is not distorted by anyone's assessment of it) is like a manhole cover lying
on the surface of the ground. People see the manhole
cover and say, "That looks like a manhole!" and Kant
says, "Yes. That cover covers a manhole of which the
bottom has never been found. You can't see the bottom of that manhole."

So someone, just to take a peek, lifts the cover and
finds nothing under it but the surface of the ground.
Kant was right in saying one could not see the bottom
of the manhole, because no one could see through the

cover. But any junior high school student could see the bottom the cover covered if the cover were removed. It would be very embarrassing to Kant to have to admit that any junior high kid could understand his unfathomable "thing in itself."

The thing in itself is objective reality. Anyone can see it, and it looks the same to all. Kant's theoretical amaurosis was due to the fact that everyone puts a unique value and a unique meaning on everything he or she sees. They all see a thing as it objectively is. Kant believed each sees things uniquely, but their divergence is in their evaluations.

456

Knowledge is neuronic impression, and learning is habit formation. Aptitude is a condition of the neurons that makes them readily impressionable.

457

A good psychoanalytic technique would be to study the pressure a person applies to a pen or pencil in writing or printing. It would show the feeling with which one expresses what one is writing - - how one feels about it. How much pressure and on what words it is applied would be revealing.

458

We never have knowledge a priori; that is knowledge prior to the experience that would teach us the knowledge. We gain the knowledge that one and one are two by very early and very elementary experience. A baby playing with blocks is soon aware that one block and another block are two blocks. This may enter his awareness via the subconscious. Perhaps that is the way all knowledge enters awareness; but it comes by way of experience. Knowledge one is born with, as knowledge of a baby to suck or of a duckling to swim, is genetic programming inherited through the experience of innumerable forebears; it is not, as Kant indicates for such concepts as time, substance, number, and causation, so reasonable as to be insinuated into the brain by simple, sheer, and plain-to-be seen obviousness.

459

As for self-consciousness in animals, to feel pain is to experience self-consciousness. Also, to feel fear makes any creature with brains conscious of itself and its predicament. Bees, in defense of their hive, or ants that panic when they smell smoke, are conscious of a peril and know they, themselves, are in it. Even the fly, which becomes evasive when the swatter misses, is conscious of his situation and knows it is himself who is in danger. The rabbit runs from the dog to save his own skin in full consciousness that it is himself he tries to save. This is action, the frankest of languages. The mouse that flees the plowman's coulter may not plan the details of his escape, but he knows the fear that makes him flee is his own impulse and that it is he who must obey it. I infer this from his actions; otherwise he would not act so; it's valid proof.

460

Natural selection endowed the crab apple with thorns, not to protect it, but because mutation made a crab apple with thorns that happened to protect it. This was by neither chance nor intention; given time, it was sure to happen.

461

To react to one visual image is *short thought*. A subject might see a banana and react by picking it up. With this he is evidencing short thought. To think short thoughts the brain need arrange no self-stimulation; the actuality of the visual image is a ready-made external stimulus. *Extended thought* is a different matter. Extended thought is creation of and reaction to mental images that are consequences of images that have gone before and causes of images that follow. To react to a mental image, the subject must first create the image. This the subject can do only indirectly, for the brain is so constituted in its function of survival faculty as to be able to affect or react to entities only exterior to itself. To induce itself to act in any way, therefore, the brain must find or create an instrument that will react upon the brain as an exterior stimulus. Speech is the ideal such instrument. By imaginatively sending out advice vocally and imaginatively receiving same aurally, the brain is able to stimulate and control itself. Eons of such employment of language has made language a genetic functionary essential to the manufacture of thought.

462

There is no reason to distinctly separate poetry and prose. If poetry is to be defined in terms of the feelings expressed and the form given the words and word groups with which the feeling is expressed, part of a line of text can be prose and part poetry. A sentence of prose may contain a phrase or clause of poetry.

463

Embarrassment necessitates self-awareness, as does guilt. I have seen ducks act out what I could characterize only as embarrassment, and a dog betrays guilt more than fear when angrily spoken to by its master. I think the many philosophers who disaffirm self-awareness in animals have not given sufficient study to the actions of animals.

464

I fail to understand how philosophers can suppose human communicable language could have been invented by a stroke of insight after man had acquired sufficient intelligence and reasoning power to appreciate syntax, parts of speech, phrase structure, etc. It seems to me that anyone familiar with human behavior must realize language evolved gradually and unconsciously from very early in man's evolution, the use of the vocal faculties becoming meaningful gradually and bit by bit over many years, every tribe developing a unique language, as the many thousands of languages extant in the world today attest.

465

Wilhelm von Humboldt (1767-1835), famous German philologist, in his seminal publication *On Language,* considers thought very sensitive to language; so, according to him, the English and the Chinese must indeed live in different worlds.

466

The fact that no word means quite the same to any two people invalidates collaboration in authorship. A single scene cannot be painted from two perspectives.

467

Money was easy to invent and to understand; for, like thought and language, it's a metaphorical phenomenon; that is, a certain amount of money is recognized as being the same as a certain amount of goods. The first question it stimulated was, "How do we get it?" Scamming was one of the first ways people thought of. The money system induces robbery; free enterprise induces sharp dealing; greed ingratiates both. *Ecce humanitas.*

468

The need to learn has an effect on learning. An animal that is raised in the safety of a human environment is unfit to survive in the wild; and a human, especially, tends to remain ignorant when the need to learn is not felt. Thus the average intelligence among humans is very low. In 1980, there were 225,048 adult people in the United States who could not read a short, simple passage and answer questions about it. Ninety-nine percent of the adults in the United States could do at least that; but 225,048 are a lot of people when you consider that elementary education is not only free, but compulsory in the United States. This reluctance to learn when the need is not felt is strikingly evident in lecture rooms of American colleges and universities.

469

Eating delicious food and having sex are two common activities that let one vividly realize the mere condition of thoroughly existing. One can get this feeling also from drugs, though transiently, and at the expense of ruining one's life.

470

Some behaviors are so genetically well programmed that they require little or no learning for their active realization. Hyperlexic children, for example, who learn to read simply by being read to while watching the text, provide evidence of how very thoroughly language has been genetically assimilated into the fabric of human thought.

471

Rules interfere with adaptation. A private language, unconsciously acquired before and after birth, follows no rules; while a common language does have rules. A common language forces more structure on one's world. It makes one's world different by diminishing its possibilities. It makes us see many of the regulatory constraints as natural impassable bulwarks, which narrows our world and inhibits our actions.

472

Psychic engulfment (one's feeling that one's world is everyone's world) is the essence of social cohesion, for the private worlds of intercommunicating people are eternal and intriguing mysteries. This makes people interesting.

473

All learning beyond the very elementary can be accomplished by reading and writing. Reading and writing should be taught on every level of education, for words are the closest things to the mind. They are essential to thought, and it is with words that we make ourselves comprehensible to others. Reading and writing are the most efficacious factors in the cultivation of man.

474

War reveals man's claim to civilization as mere affectation. But for social structure man would be no more civilized than a beast of the jungle.

475

Overeating is the deadliest vice. As a consequence of overeating, hypertension and excessive cholesterol kill many; and addiction to food is impossible to abate because one cannot totally abstain.

476

The trouble with learning about people through texts taught by teachers is that teachers give one a limited view of people and so one finds them uninteresting. One should carefully read the writings of the people themselves. I have, until now (at the age of eighty-six), thought of John Locke as being an enthusiastic supporter of the American Revolution and not much else. On reading the words he wrote, I find he died the greater part of a century before the Revolutionary War. Locke's philosophy in the American Revolution, like Hegel's in the Russian Revolution, was used as palliation to comfort the effects of the primitive slaughter of war. Hegel died eighty-six years before the Russian revolution.

477

What is there about priority that gives one a natural right to something? Might is the only natural right. All else are man-made rules, and even they have to be enforced with might.

478

Locke, who was smarting from heavy taxation, said man's natural rights are life, liberty, and property. Jefferson, who had to countenance the robbery of North America from the Indians, said man's natural rights are life, liberty, and the pursuit of happiness. Here we see how reason caters to desire.

479

To learn, we focus attention and achieve understanding, then we repeatedly present and review the subject material. We should learn this process; then, from kindergarten to PHD, we should study the meanings of words; for that is the key that opens the door to all learning.

480

To be mentally processable a concept must be made concrete by imaging, realizable to the senses, stimulating; that is, to certain nerves. There is nothing magic about the mind. Without imagery, the mind would have nothing to think about. Words received from a communicatee evoke images in the mind of their recipient; and images concretize concepts, giving meaning to words. All thinkers, even the congenitally blind, think with imagery (see Stephen Kosslyn, *Image and Brain,* page 335). Philosophers and mathematicians use words (for numbers and symbols are also words) as concrete stepping stones in their progress from problem to solution. If philosophers and mathematicians could think in the abstract, they would not need words. Imagery is the bridge across the abyss of abstraction.

481

At about 300 B.C. the ancient Greeks achieved a perfect system of pure logic by transcending reality. This stopped the progress of knowledge until Galileo (1564-1642). Just so would a species adapted perfectly to its environment soon become extinct; for adaptation comes of disorder, not order.

482

The talk about the wish to stop war is a great hypocrisy. War is our favorite sport, more exciting than football. Music is used to incite the soldier, and rules are made for the way the game is played. War is suffused with the glow of romance; it reifies the essence of comradeship; young men relish the opportunity of showing themselves brave; war draws the citizenry together in a thrilling orgy of sympathy, grief, and glory that transcends all pettiness; it clears out the dusty tedium of years of everyday life; it taps our primitive animal urges; and with all the vibrant energy of life, we live.

483

It's a kind of suicide not to use your mind to a full and satisfying extent. Your mind is you. Your consciousness is your life and the use of it is living. When you miss a chance to think creatively, a part of you is wasted; some of your life has been destroyed. It's a kind of suicide also not to learn all you can, not to go to school.

484

The versatility of language and the degree of dexterity in the use of it to which lawyers have been trained allow a lawyer pleading a case to commit legally an act that, if committed by a common citizen out of court, would be a punishable offense. Once, in the course of a trial in which I was a member of that jury, a lawyer said, "Take a good look at my client; I hope you will not allow his formidable appearance to intimidate you." The formidable appearance of the client, the imperative intimation of the clause "Take a good look" and the uncalled-for-raising of the issue mark this lawyer's sentence a veiled threat. The way it is put, however, makes it unlikely to incite an objection. In any case, a sustained objection would probably result, at most, in the judge's request that the jury forget the disapproved implication. This, of course, would be impossible.

This breach of justice could be prevented by using written pleas purged of such suasion by the opposing lawyer under supervision of the presiding judge.

485

Because one percent of the world's population are thought to be schizophrenic, it was judged that schizophrenia must have some survival value; and this was found indeed to be so. The schizophrenic was found to be abler than the mentally sound person to survive burns. I believe mitral valve prolapse could be found far more probably to have a like value; for it has been found that approximately seventy percent of the population of North America are thought to have prolapse of the mitral valve. If this condition has survived in man to such an extent, it must have evolved as a safety valve to prevent the force of the blood pushed from the left ventricle into the arteries from being too great during moments of great physical stress. If, for example, a human had to run from an animal or an enemy till nearly exhausted and then had to hide and be extremely quiet to avoid detection—which must have been a fairly common experience for man during his evolution—the force of the heartbeat would be very, very strong for a while. It is for this reason that athletes need to "walk it off" after a race. If the mitral valve lets a little blood back into the left atrium, a great deal of pressure is taken off the arteries, thereby reducing the danger of stroke.

486

In reference to the optic disk (also called "blind spot") in the field of vision, the brain does not, as believed by many, fill in the blind spot fictively to simulate completeness. Imagine the field of vision of each eye divided into thirds. With both eyes open, the two left thirds of the right eye's field of vision and the two right thirds of the left eye's field of vision overlap. This overlap contains the blind spot of each eye; so that while both eyes are open there is no blind spot; for, because the two blind spots do not occlude the same area, each eye can see the area occluded by the other. If one eye is closed, the area occluded by the blind spot of the open eye is again occluded. This acquits the brain of a deception that would have amounted to a hazardous situation and that natural selection, which preserves only the fittest, would have been unable to make the brain capable.

487

The Japanese child gets little or none of the boredom Bertrand Russell finds essential to happiness, as almost every free minute of a Japanese childhood and youth is taken up in some sort of group activity. Individuality is discouraged where nearness makes provocation more cutting and reverberatory. In Japan, a child who is a standout because of being superior to others is considered an abnormality that has to be normalized. This homogenization prevents the complexities of comparison, resentment, shame, and discouragement that prevail among the losers in the USA, where excelling over others is always applauded and who rate down toward the middle in the world for academic excellence. The crowded conditions of the Japanese, who always rate among the top in the world for academic excellence, make celebration of superiority more poignantly painful to the losers than the same in a more thinly populated country, where a loser can find privacy in which to nurse his wounds and learn to accept his inferiority and avoid competition.

488

In the remote future, providing the earth still harbors the human species, how primitive we shall appear when students consider our current way of choosing the waste of war where reasonable conciliation so obviously belongs!

489

The traveling of an electrochemically conducted impulse over a neuronal route in the brain is the action essential to sensation; and the immediate traveling of an electrochemically conducted impulse back over the same route, known as reentry, is the action essential to consciousness. Reentry, incited by the energy aroused by sensation, causes consciousness. Consciousness is the sensing of sensation.

490

Uncountable centuries have so diffused the custom of war throughout man's culture that he is blind to the glaring fact that war between humans, who possess empathy, sympathy, reasoning ability, and general intelligence, is an absurd anachronism. It's by no means necessary, for man could very handily settle his national differences in a world-government court of law. War is of use only to military industrialists, who make an exorbitant superfluity of money by the manufacture of lethal weapons.

In a plutocracy such as the United States of America, whose members of government are allowed to accept any amount of money from any donor, the lives of our youth are fuel to feed the engines of greed.

All nations that use money, rest assured, are plutocracies. Money, invented to facilitate the acquisition of the necessities of life, because of its extreme versatility, quickly became the object for which the necessities of life, and even life itself, are spent - - - the object, in fact, for whose acquisition the lives of thousands of youths are swept away like noisome insects. It's murder for money in mastodonic degree.

All humans, in general, are people just like other people. Counsel and compromise between people can be accomplished. Why resort to murder?

INDEX

END